Anglican and Puritan

Anglican and Puritan

The Basis of Their Opposition, 1558–1640

John F. H. New

1964
Stanford University Press
Stanford, California

Stanford University Press
Stanford, California
© 1964 by the Board of Trustees of the
Leland Stanford Junior University
All rights reserved
Library of Congress Catalog Card Number: 64-12075
Printed in the United States of America

Acknowledgments

In writing this book I have incurred many debts:

To the Canadian Universities' Foundation for electing me Commonwealth Research Fellow for two years, during which time I undertook a Ph.D. program at the University of Toronto. The present study has evolved from my dissertation.

To Elliot Rose of the University of Toronto, and in particular to my distinguished supervisor, A. S. P. Woodhouse, for trenchant criticism and keen interest.

To George Yule of the University of Melbourne, who first kindled my interest in the Tudor and Stuart field.

To Donald N. Baker for reading the manuscript as it came from the desk.

To J. G. Bell, Mary Johnson, and Pauline Wickham, of Stanford University Press, for helping me prepare the book for publication.

And to my wife for her cheerful support.

To all these I am grateful, and to many friends who go unnamed.

J. F. H. N.

Contents

One must clearly either accept [the Christian] "myth" as history itself, and call all other histories myth, or otherwise refuse the Christian "myth" and remain with the human notion of history.

The Christian Church confesses that this "myth" is history itself. She recognizes herself by this myth, she recognizes her life, her true reality. She is the witness of witnesses, she recognizes through the Holy Spirit that this is the one really interesting story. Then she turns back the historians' weapon: She says to them: What you call "myth," that is history! She will also add: What you call history, that is a myth! A myth, a made-up history, that fancies the fate of man as depending on his earthly vicissitudes, a myth, a made-up history, that confuses the immediate success of a cause with its truth, and so on.

KARL BARTH, The Faith and the Church

> One's grand flights, one's Sunday baths,
> One's tootings at the weddings of the soul
> Occur as they occur. So bluish clouds
> Occurred above the empty house and the leaves
> Of the rhododendrons rattled their gold,
> As if someone lived there. Such floods of white
> Came bursting from the clouds. So the wind
> Threw its contorted strength around the sky.
> Could you have said the blue-jay suddenly
> Would swoop to earth? It is a wheel, the rays
> Around the sun. The wheel survives the myths.
> The fire eye in the clouds survives the gods.
> To think of a dove with an eye of grenadine
> And pines that are cornets, so it occurs,
> And a little island full of geese and stars.

WALLACE STEVENS, The Sense of the Sleight-of-hand Man

All human discourse is metaphorical. . . . In what sense can myths and metaphors be true or false? In the sense that . . . they may report the general movement and the pertinent issue of the material facts, and may inspire us with a wise sentiment in their presence.

GEORGE SANTAYANA, <i>Some Turns of Thought in Modern Philosophy</i>

Anglican and Puritan

Introduction

The method of this book is analytical rather than chronological. I have not undertaken to trace the continuity and change, the modification and strengthening, of the religious attitudes concerned. And, because historians are familiar with the main developments within the Church during the century before the Civil War, I give no systematic account of the widening rift between the Anglican and the Puritan groups, of the particular issues and controversies as they successively emerged. As Sir Walter Raleigh wrote in prefacing his history, "Seeing therein I should but borrow other men's words, I will not trouble the reader with the repetition." If a story is an integral part of a history, here is no history. There is, however, an attempt to uncover characteristic attitudes and to explain them from a religious point of view. Hopefully, the result will be less a monistic explanation than a contribution to a synthesis that has not yet been written.

It follows that our findings will be in some degree speculative and impressionistic; they are offered as hypotheses, no more than that. The argument deliberately emphasizes one aspect of a many-sided theme because this facet has been neglected (and also because it interests me), and trusts there may be virtue in self-conscious partiality.

Definitions are mandatory in any study of Puritan-Anglican opposition. In such a complex science as history it is more appropriate that definitions be useful than perfectly precise. So, instead of qualifying the terms to the point of cumbrousness, I have reduced them to "working" definitions, even though their application obscures the shades of meaning, the blurred and ragged edges between the classifications.

Before we start, however, a purist may cry that the word Puritan cannot be applied, say, to Thomas Cartwright, who objected to the epithet. He might add that the Five Dissenting Brethren of the Westminster Assembly were not prepared to accept the label Independent until after the *Apologetical Narration* of 1644. Levellers also resented their nickname. The objection is noteworthy but should not hold us up. We know whom we mean because we have enlarged the contemporary definitions by purging them of the smears and implications that Cartwright, the Independents, and the Levellers resented (treason, separatism, and "socialism," respectively); so we can safely impose our definitions upon the unwilling participants of the time.

The word Anglican is used here to include those generally satisfied with the Church's doctrine, organization, and ceremonial. It excludes those Puritans who, though members of the Establishment, wanted alterations in Church ritual or Church government, or both. And Puritan, as it is used here, excludes those who hoped to dissociate the Church from the State. These definitions sacrifice a little breadth for greater clarity. Our dividing line is drawn between the Independents and the Separatists, an arbitrary line, to be sure, and an unsatisfactory one in many ways. Independency and Presbyterianism shared profound cosmic assumptions with groups of "the left," but kept tight rein on the consequences of their ideas in the interests of social stability. If at times we emphasize the bonds between Anglican and Puritan, that is only one side, albeit an important side, of the coin. Whenever distinctions between the two are made—and that is the heart of our intention—the Puritan view belongs also to the Sects; and though attention has not been drawn to every carry-over on the way, it may be taken for granted by the reader.

Both a thesis and an antithesis lie within Puritanism: along with a conservative desire to remain a church-type institution, it contained factors undermining that urge. One should not attempt a synthesis of these tendencies because it is truer to fact to leave them in an unresolved tension, fighting a constant tug-of-war with each other. In the century from Archbishop Cranmer to Archbishop Laud it was this type of Puritanism, and not Separatism, that threatened the Establishment. These Puritans who were not Sectaries constituted a greater danger to the

Church order than the Separatists, whose influence was only peripheral until the Civil War created the conditions that lent them relevance to their time. Thus, while I have tried to leave Puritanism suspended in its own stresses, I feel justified in limiting the term to those who rejected the Separatists' departure from the State Church. At this point, then, our definition of Puritan is in secular and governmental terms. By the end of the study, however, Puritan will be defined in terms of underlying attitudes. Although it may sound curious to begin with one definition and end with another, new possibilities can only be explored from the launching pad of accepted ideas.

Over the years a body of historical judgments has grown to such maturity and eminence that most students defer to it: tensions arose during and after the Settlement because some felt the Elizabethan Church sufficiently reformed, whereas others thought it insufficiently scriptural. At first the Puritans wanted minor vestiarian alterations, but frustration moved them toward more ambitious ends. In the mid-1560's, a "prophesying mission" (a system of seminars in Biblical exegesis) sprang up to educate preaching ministers. Then an attack was launched upon the structure of Church government itself: meetings of presbyteries, called classes, were grafted onto episcopacy in order to supplant it, but John Whitgift crushed this scheme. Puritanism then lapsed into quiescence until James's accession (1603). Failing to gain satisfaction from him, harried by that energetic Anglican, Richard Bancroft, and shocked at Court life, it vented its energy in formal moralism. Matters might have stood there but for William Laud's consolidation in power. The novel practices enforced by him provoked another onslaught against episcopacy, culminating in 1645 in its temporary deposition by the Long Parliament for the duration of the Interregnum. Behind this long struggle the crucial issue at stake was the authority of the Church, and ultimately the royal supremacy in the State as well as the Church.

This interpretation confuses means with ends. It has developed because historians have looked at the problem of the Church from a predominantly political standpoint—a reflex of modern secularism. Thus the Church has been woven into the fabric of constitutional history as an institution of State, which it was and which it was not. The process forgets that the Church was a reservoir of faith and ideas, the oracle of an eternal *kerygma*. So, in a broad sense, this book pleads a case against too secular a description of the Elizabethan and early Stuart religious struggles. Of course some studies suffer an opposite defect, being concerned purely with 'theological taxonomy. Among historians, however, the common practice has been to cast Anglicans and Puritans as ecclesiastical politicians playing the game for the sake of power. Mine is an attempt to enter the minds of the antagonists by an ideological approach; and from this angle the retention or removal of vestments, the conservation or reconstruction of Church polity, the flexibility or rigidity of the moral order, and the defense or trespass of the royal prerogative were not ends in themselves, but teleological acts—attempts to make practice conform to preconceived philosophies.

The habit of regarding the actions of Anglicans and Puritans as the ends in themselves has encouraged inadequate assessments of the thought and motivation of both parties. Viewed in this light, their behavior often seems petty and malign. This view errs, too, in assuming that the differences were merely over matters of government and ritual, scriptural uses against traditional forms, when, in fact, subtle doctrinal differences existed from the outset and became more apparent over the years. These differences amounted to alien "universes of discourse," to use philosophers' jargon, from which the shifting conflicts emerged and re-emerged, and it is these dogmatic bases of opposition that invite closer attention.

Chapter 1 Man

Man has sought to discover the purpose of his life on earth and the future thereafter since he first became aware of his mortality. The odyssey is endless, and men's theodicy will probably continue as long as the species lasts. In our time the recourse to gods or God has proved less popular than previously; yet despite the profusion of modern alternatives, we might venture that man's relationship to God has been the dominant motif of Western thought for two millennia.

In general, moreover, it has been possible to identify two strains in man's view of life, an optimistic and a tragic view, although the two are not so distinct as we sometimes imagine. In our zeal for clarity we tend to credit the Greeks with optimism and rationalism, and to heap responsibility for the disavowal of human potential onto the heads of the Hebrews. Both civilizations nurtured both traits. Although Pythagoras claimed that man was the measure of all things, and Phidias placed idealized god-men and god-women upon pedestals, the tragedians Sophocles and Thucydides represent a more melancholy strain. In Judeo-Christianity, the later and lesser prophets voiced naïve hopes for the Kingdom of Heaven on earth, and the Synoptic Gospels proclaimed the availability of salvation in return for free repentance and simple trust. They preached the possibility of a life of virtue in the footsteps of Jesus Christ. Ironically it was the Hellenized St. Paul and the author of the fourth Gospel who interpolated a sense of the gravity of the human predicament into the New Testament. The counter tendency, however, had indigenous Hebrew roots in the Book of Job. Its post-exilic author changed an old legend, possibly the fatalistic Mesopotamian myth called Ludlul bel Nemequi, into a thoroughgoing elaboration of the doctrine of original sin by adding the speeches of Elihu. Since then the notion of innate depravity has been a potent element in man's aspiration for the transcendent, and a ground for his frenetic clamor for absolution from his feelings of guilt.

Meaning, destiny, sin, and salvation: the questions are perennial. Yet within one heritage the slightest deviation has precipitated estrangements and promoted violently contradictory groupings of belief and action. The Emperor Constantine's calling of the Council of Nicaea (325) to resolve the Church's dispute with Arius is a classic example of what massive consequences can hang upon one letter of a single word. The question then was the consubstantiality (*homoiousia*) or the similarity (*homoousia*) of the Son and the Father in the Person of the Trinity. Upon the outcome of this question, the unity of Christendom, and perhaps the vitality of the Roman Empire, depended. Though less dramatic and specific, our problem is analogous; for Anglicanism and Puritanism stood in the same field of the Reformation, sharing the earthly and contingent pessimism that had originated in Judaism and had been reaffirmed by St. Paul, St. Augustine, John Wycliffe, Luther, Calvin, Martin Bucer, and Peter Martyr. Both Anglicans and Puritans accepted the doctrine of total depravity, the Fall from Grace, and its attendant consequence, the doctrine of justification by faith alone. Yet variations within the same broad framework—even under the rubric of identical statements of doctrine—gave rise to behavior patterns that at times became diametrically opposed. Even small distinctions aroused antagonism because the subtleties were meaningful to those who lived and felt them.

Anglicans and Puritans lived and felt their religion. They varied minutely in their measurement of man's fall at the Fall; and their answers involved different views of human nature in general. Anglicans found that though Adam's fall had emasculated his spiritual capability, not every faculty for good had been crushed out of him. Man was sorely wounded with sin, but not so critically as the Puritans claimed. Anglicanism allowed man an unimpaired power of natural reason—natural reason being the capacity to judge and to perform good and evil as reckoned by a moral order in the world whose existence neither side questioned.

The whole of humanity was comprehended in a spiritual infirmity that was both inherited and inherent. The Litany branded everyone a "miserable sinner,"[1] and, according to Hugh Latimer, even the Virgin Mary was not without a "sparkle of sin."[2] At times the pronouncements of Anglican clerics seem grotesque and exaggerated, as Lancelot Andrewes' contrast between men and angels: "Corruption and rottenness, and worms. They, glorious Spirits; we vile bodies . . . and not only base and vile, but filthy and unclean." He denigrated man to "a thing of nought,"[3] and he did this by means of physical images. The contexts of these overall indictments of sinfulness need to be examined carefully to determine whether sin is imputed as a spiritual or as a worldly attribute. When, in a sermon, Edwin Sandys announced that man was free only to do evil, he must be understood in the theological sense.[4] Man's attempts to reach salvation were so infected with pride that he was ever inclined to err and to stray from the true way of redemption.[5] Sandys was not condemning every earthbound action; he was stressing the doctrinal point that original sin so limited a man's understanding that he became spiritually impotent, and all his efforts were insufficient for salvation.[6]

Notwithstanding this absolute spiritual deficiency, the Fall had not erased a natural ability to reason. Within an earthly context, man was capable of choosing the good. The word "good" in this sense was used morally and sociologically in an area unrelated to redemption. Thomas Cranmer, for instance, assumed that men could choose the good without the help of actual or sanctifying grace when he approved St. Chrysostom's dictum that "you shall find many which have not the true faith, and be not of the flock of Christ, and yet (as it appeareth) they flourish in good works of mercy; you shall find them full of pity, compassion, and given to justice; and yet for all that they have not fruit of their works because the chief work lacketh." And Cranmer paraphrased: "He that doth good deeds, yet without faith, he hath not life."⁷ In other words, a man could act well under the spur of his own nature, even though he would never achieve everlasting life.

Calvin, by contrast, severely limited the powers of natural reason. The Fall did not wholly destroy man's intelligence, which remained to give some measure of direction to "mechanical arts and liberal studies" and "civil order and honesty."⁸ The Fall did not so much destroy as pervert the intellectual apparatus. "Our souls are a very abyss of iniquity."⁹ "We are so utterly mastered under the power of sin that our whole mind, heart, and all our actions bend towards sin." Calvin denied the possibility of an "intermediate nature"; "the whole nature is, as it were, a seed bed of sin" in which "perversity never ceases."¹⁰ Reason remained, but as an enfeebled and distorted remnant of Adam's pristine integrity.

The dissonance between Cranmer and Calvin echoed and re-echoed in the subsequent conflict. Sometimes, in Anglican pronouncements, the ability for valid thinking is implied or even stated, as it was by Roger Goad, Vice-Chancellor of the University of Cambridge. Correcting an errant divinity lecturer in 1595, he maintained that "out of the church, the Turks, and other barbarous nations . . . had external gifts common to this life, granted them by God; yet they were altogether destitute of grace sufficient to salvation."¹¹ John Jewel made his recognition of reason quite explicit when he commented on Alexander Severus's arbitration of a dispute over a plot of land: the Emperor had decided rightly, "being a heathen, and void of faith, and led only by the guiding of nature." Again, Jewel was convinced that American Indians would distinguish correctly between the English and Roman religions out of innate perspicacity. "I doubt not but nature herself would lead them to judge that ours is light and yours darkness."¹² Similarly, Andrewes admitted man's ability for valid choosing. "Now then, this is the rule of reason, the guide of all choice, evermore to take the better and leave the worse. This would man do. *Haec est lex hominis*."¹³ And Laud thought that the use of reason was one method of proving the Scriptures to be the Word of God. "Give even natural reason

leave to come in, and make some proof, and make sure approbation upon the weighing and considering of the arguments.
And this [proof] must be admitted, if it be but for pagans and
infidels."[14] Finally, of course, the breadth of the domain that
Richard Hooker left to reason needs no comment. These men,
different in temperament and living at different times, agreed
upon a fundamental faith in man's moral effectiveness in this
world, despite original sin.

Conversely, Puritanism interpreted the Fall as total perversion. William Perkins described the event as "a revolting of the
reasonable creature from obedience to sin," and he defined sin
as having two parts: "A defect, or impotence; and disorder. Impotence is nothing else but the very want or loss of that good,
which God hath ingrafted in the very nature of his creatures."
Up to this point, Perkins was describing a spiritual defect, and
his position here was in complete agreement with Anglicanism.
But he continued: "Disorder is the confusion or disturbance of
all the powers and actions of the creature."[15] Like Calvin, he believed in man's total corruption. "Original sin is nothing else,
but a disorder or evil disposition in all the faculties and inclina-
tions of men, whereby they are all carried inordinately against
the law of God. The subject or place of this sin, is not any part
of man, but the whole body and soul. For first of all, the natural
appetite to meat and drink, and the power of nourishing is
greatly corrupted . . . Secondly, the outward senses are as corrupt . . . Thirdly, touching the understanding, the spirit of
God sayeth, that the frame of the heart of man is only evil continually: so we are not able of our selves to think a good
thought."[16]

Perkins, the most outstanding systematic Puritan theologian
of his time, is echoed by other Elizabethan writers. Richard
Rogers, for example, discounted natural faculties in similar
terms. "Regeneration," he wrote, "is a spiritual birth of the
whole man, which is, whereas the natural faculties of the soul,
as Reason, Understanding, Will, Affection, and the members of
the body also, are so sanctified and purged by grace that we
understand, will and desire that which is good: for till a man

be born again, he can no more desire that which is good, than a dead man can desire the good things in this life."[17] In these passages the word "good" is used in both a spiritual and an earthly sense. The whole man was gripped and controlled by sin. But, as with Anglicans so with Puritans, we must draw meticulous distinctions; for Puritans did not deny that man had knowledge of good and evil—that would be to deny the Fall—rather, they asserted a total inability in man to desire and to choose rightly, and in that lay their alienation from Anglicanism.

Not only was man's mental faculty incapable of achieving earthly good; it actively hindered his chances of attaining heavenly truth. Man's pretensions were so stuffed with pride that they did dishonor to God, and any tendency to rely on reason was a movement away from the humility required for godly repentance. As Calvin had seen, a recourse to reason amounted to a declaration that some undefiled ability existed in man as man, a claim that was arrogant, unthankful, and self-glorifying—the quintessence of sin. "Man cannot arrogate to himself one particle beyond his due, without losing himself in vain confidence, and by transferring divine honour to himself, becoming guilty of the greatest impiety. And assuredly whenever our minds are seized with a longing to possess somewhat of our own which may reside in us rather than in God, we may rest assured that the thought is suggested by no other counsellor than he who enticed our first parents to aspire to be like God."[18] An Elizabethan Puritan put it pithily: "The leaven of old Adam is in us, and maketh us swell in pride; and such is the foolish pride of our hearts, that we care least for God."[19] Similarly, the preacher Thomas Adams described pride as "a subtle insinuating sin . . . no sin is more saucy; none more bold with God, none less welcome."[20] Pride was the rub; man retained his judgment of good and evil, but his desires and designs, all his motives in fact, were basically evil.

Since reason represented a built-in temptation of the mind, Puritanism tended to distrust it in any form. Whitgift's polemical habits horrified Cartwright, not because Whitgift had the better of the exchanges, but because "there is some star of light or reason, or learning, or other help, whereby some act may be well done and acceptably unto God, in which the word of God was shut out, and not called to counsel."[21] In the next century, Anthony Tuckney's letters (1651) to Benjamin Whichcote display a deep suspicion of philosophy and learning;[22] and Oliver Cromwell's hesitations to rely on reason peep through the Putney Debates (1647) and glare through his speeches to the Protectorate parliaments.[23] His increasing justification by Providence and Necessity indicates the extent of his want of confidence in "fleshly reasonings," as he called them.[24]

For Anglicanism, rational thought was God's handmaiden, ranking lower than faith, but a noble gift nonetheless. Cranmer trusted that "although our sense can not reach so far as faith doth; yet so far as the compass of our sense doth usually reach our faith is not contrary to the same but rather our senses do confirm our faith."[25] How close Cranmer's view was to Hooker's! "St. Paul teacheth . . . that nature hath need of grace, whereunto I hope we are not opposite in holding that grace hath use of nature."[26] That natural faculties were not hindrances but the helpmates of God was certainly Jewel's opinion: "Natural reason holden within her bounds is not the enemy, but the daughter of God's truth."[27] And John Donne had a similar attitude, for when Scripture seemed obscure he said we should approach it with human reason. "Though our supreme court . . . for the last Appeal be Faith, yet Reason is her delegate."[28] Puritanism found reason a deranged *imago dei,* twisted against Him and not to be trusted, whereas, within mundane bounds, Anglicanism vaunted the ability to choose the good, and claimed that reason was a fit complement to faith.

This does not mean, however, that Anglicans believed in free will for salvation. The point has already been made, but it should be repeated because the concept of free will attracts confusion. In part, the difficulties arise when finite activity becomes muddled with infinite affairs. Anglicanism accepted man's freedom of choice within earthly bounds, whereas Puritanism qualified this by accounting all motives evil. Where redemption was concerned, both Anglican and Puritan agreed that man was neither "master of his fate" nor "captain of his soul." He was destined for death unless he received everlasting life through the pure and unwarranted gift of sanctifying grace. As God's love was not negotiable and salvation could not be solicited, so worldly freedom was irrelevant to eternal judgment. Though Anglicanism allowed of choice in the finite realm, it disallowed it altogether in the sphere of the infinite.

If justification by faith alone is a hallmark of Protestantism, the Church of England was unequivocally Protestant, and its basic Protestantism ought to be firmly grasped before we proceed to the modifications. This essential, however, has been blurred by the use of the term *via media* to describe the Elizabethan Settlement.[29] The term obscures the issue, since its comfortable generality seems to render a scrupulous examination unnecessary, and as a result we fail to get a true perspective. Only when we have recognized that the Settlement was unequivocally Protestant does it become proper to point out the Roman Catholic undertones, one of which was the Anglicans' trust in reason.

That Anglicanism renounced spiritual free will can be effectively illustrated by citing two "notorious Arminians." Andrewes' comment on the second of the Lambeth Articles is self-explanatory. "The moving, or efficient, cause of predestination to life is not prevenient faith, or perseverance, or good works, or any other thing that is innate in the predestined person, but only the will of a beneficent God."[30] Or, in a sermon: "We are regenerate by the rising again of Christ;—right. As to death generate by the Fall of the first Adam, so to life regenerate by the rising again of Christ, the second." "We have it [salvation] not of ourselves, or by our merits, by the πολύ [abundance?] of them; but of Him, and by His mercies, and the πολύ of them; else were it a purchase, and no inheritance. It comes to us freely, as the inheritance to children."[31] Laud was equally adamant. "Man lost by sin the integrity of his nature, and can not have light enough to see the way to heaven but by grace. This grace was first merited, after given, by Christ; this grace is just kindled by faith, [without] which . . . we can never see our way." Furthermore, "fundamental points of faith, without which there is no salvation . . . can not be proved by reason."[32] Both Puritan and Anglican alike affirmed that salvation was entirely God's business, and that freedom belonged to Him alone and was not an attribute of man.

Some Anglicans, however, softened the rigor of predestination in the interests of God's universal charity. The doctrine of predestination, or rather that form of it which interests historians, had a two-way application (hence it is sometimes called double predestination). Some were chosen to eternal bliss, and others were relegated to everlasting perdition. "From eternity God has predestined some to life and reprobated others to death" runs the first of the Lambeth Articles.[33] Article XVII of the Church of England, however, does not specify that God decreed the non-elect to damnation, though it is implied. Some Anglicans resolutely refused to recognize the implication. Andrewes thought that attributing reprobation to a decree of God came perilously close to making God responsible for sin. God was benign and loving, and man was reprobated for his want of belief. An undercurrent of grace flowed in all men, and salvation was proffered to all if not conferred on all. That some missed their heaven-sent opportunity was not due to God's inexorable will but to human obstinacy. This may appear to release a trickle of free will in the form of an accepting or rejecting power in man. But Andrewes allowed no power of choice whatsoever with respect to spiritual good, until grace had first removed the impediments and provided the strength for perseverance. God alone could supply the necessary prevenient grace.

Freedom remained, then, only in the ability to revert to obstinacy: that is, man's free will could affect nothing but evil. This was Arminianism.* The difference between the Lambeth Articles and Andrewes' judgment upon them was that the former asserted that the elect would become believers, and the latter that all those who believed were the true elect.[34] Christ died for all, not just for the elect; sanctifying grace was resistible; and the believer, like Esau, could despise and reject his inheri-

---

* The doctrine was propounded in 1589 by the celebrated Dutch theologian Jacobus Arminius. See A. W. Harrison, *The Beginnings of Arminianism to the Synod of Dort* (London, 1926), or James Hastings, ed., *Encyclopedia of Religion and Ethics* (New York, 1951).

tance. The controversy over Arminianism in the University of Cambridge in 1595 reveals that Andrewes, William Barrett, Peter Baro, John Overall, and a host of other prominent Anglicans were, in the strict theological sense, Arminians.[35] (Since the Council of Orange in 529 this construction of sin and grace had been normative in Christianity, in both Protestantism and Roman Catholicism. Among Separatists the position was maintained by the General Baptists as distinct from the Particular Baptists.) But free will to act righteously in a spiritual context was beyond all controversy, save in the misrepresentations of anti-Arminians several decades later.[36]

Although Arminianism had a legitimate birth in theology, the epithet lost its proper application when it became popular as a catch-cry in the 1620's, a quarter of a century after the scuffle about it at Cambridge was done. Events in Holland, combined with new emphases in the Church at home, revived the issue and made it topical. In 1618, the Dutch Arminians (or Remonstrants) had been expelled by the Synod of Dort, so the epithet, by association, linked English Arminians with heresy. Since some semi-Pelagian Roman Catholics (after Erasmus) upheld free will for salvation, opponents misassociated Arminianism with Popery. And James I's distaste for the Remonstrants—he sent a handpicked delegation, headed by the Irish theologian James Ussher, to oppose them at Dort—gave support to the additional insinuation that Arminians, like the Dutch heretics, formed a disruptive and dissident faction within the nation—a charge that turned old Anglican thrusts at the Puritans back against the Arminians with brilliant irony. It was, in short, a propaganda windfall that very soon crystallized into established conviction.

Unfortunately *The Dictionary of English Church History* offers a misleading definition: "Arminianism is a general term used to cover the whole high church and latitudinarian reaction against the intellectual tyranny of Calvinism."[37] The use of post–Civil War labels (high church and latitudinarian) for pre–Civil War attitudes is inept; and the concluding phrase implies that Calvinism was dominant within the Church until the reaction, a view that this study as a whole attempts to refute.

In actual usage the epithet became inseparably linked with Popery. In a Remonstrance of 1628, the Commons noted "with sorrow . . . a daily growth and spreading of the faction of the Arminians, that being, as your Majesty well knows, a cunning way to bring in Popery, and the professors of this opinion [are] the common disturbers of Protestant churches and incendiaries in those states wherein they have gotten any head, being Protestants in show, but Jesuits in opinion . . . who, notwithstanding, are much favored and advanced, not wanting friends even of the clergymen to your Majesty, namely Dr. Neale, Bishop of Winchester, and Dr. Laud, Bishop of Bath and Wells, who are justly suspected to be unsound in their opinions that way."[38] (Yet doctrinally Laud, at least, was not an unqualified Arminian.[39]) The Resolutions of the Commons of 1629 treated Popery as interchangeable with Arminianism. "Whoever shall bring an innovation of religion, or by favour or countenance seek to extend or introduce popery or Arminianism, or other opinion disagreeing from the true and orthodox church, shall be a capital enemy to this Kingdom and Commonwealth."[40] The term by then had lost trace of its theological origin. It applied to all who maintained the semblance of Romanism: to believers in a decorous ceremonial; to advocates of a meticulous outward uniformity; and to defenders of a strict hierarchical polity. In other words, it was used as a gibe at rigid churchmanship, and variations over predestination had little to do with the matter.[41]

Predestination was a minor doctrine, correlated to justification by faith alone, and to God's sovereignty. It did not encourage Antinomianism because gratitude for God's justification, and obedience to His absolute will, prevented the concept of assurance (the belief that salvation was assured) from getting out of control.* Calvin had elaborated on the principle of double predestination in the *Institutes* (1536),† but treated it as a de-

---

* Antinomianism is the belief that the moral law is not binding on Christians because it is abrogated by the inspiration of grace.
† Calvin wrote the *Institutes* in Latin in 1535, they were published in 1536, and the first translation, in French, was issued in 1540.

rivative doctrine, as is clear from the inconsequential place it holds in Book III, and from his statement that "we shall never feel persuaded as we ought that our salvation flows from the free mercy of God, as its fountain, until we are made acquainted with his eternal election, the grace of God being illustrated by the contrast. . . . It is plain how greatly ignorance of this principle detracts from the glory of God and impairs true humility."[42] To Calvin, a double decree seemed necessary to understand God's love and omnipotence; it was both a logical consequence and an illustration of greater truths. This view was shared by Perkins, who began his *Treatise on Predestination* (1598) by observing that "the supreme end of predestination is the manifestation of God's glory, partly in his mercy, and partly in his justice."[43] And he closed a passage on reprobation by stressing that "this is the full exercise of God's decree of reprobation, whereby appeareth the great justice of God in punishing sin: from whence also cometh God's glory, which he propoundeth to himself as the last and chiefest end in all these things. Therefore, let every Christian propound the same end unto himself."[44]

When Calvin set out the ten fundamentals of his creed for the Protector Somerset, he did not mention predestination.[45] He never preached about it, and, like Luther, he warned that the problem ought to be handled with extreme delicacy.[46] In view of the evidence, it is strange that historians have been so dogmatic.

Whitgift's belief in predestination has been widely misconstrued to mean that his quarrel with Cartwright was non-doctrinal.* Biographers have assumed that Whitgift was a moderate Calvinist who differed from the Puritans only in his staunch advocacy of the Anglican system. According to one account, he "remained in theory well disposed to those portions of the Calvinist doctrine which did not touch ritual or discipline." Similarly, A. F. Scott Pearson, the great authority on Cartwright, judged that "Cartwright's quarrel with the English

---

* For a discussion of the Whitgift-Cartwright controversy, see pp. 64 and 105 below.

Church [that is, with Whitgift] was not a theological one."[47] The conclusion that Whitgift was a Calvinist rests on the Lambeth Articles and a brief statement about the certainty of salvation; it merits close attention because it forms an indispensable prop for a larger and popular view of Elizabethan Church history.

Given the Calvinism of Anglicanism, the squabbles between Anglican and Puritan have to be interpreted as administrative, or temperamental, or economic in origin, rather than doctrinal. This interpretation, with Whitgift's Calvinism as its *ratio decidendi,* has become the established one, despite the fact that it colligates three errors. First, it assumes that predestination was a major article of faith for Whitgift, when it was not. In the letter he sent, together with the Articles of 1595, to the Heads of the Colleges, he asked them to see to it not only that "nothing should be publicly taught to the contrary," but also that "discretion and moderation should be used; that such as should be in some points differing in judgment, might not be of purpose stung or justly grieved. And especially that no bitterness, contentions, or personal reproof or reproaches, should be used by any toward any." The propositions were only "private judgments . . . and not laws and decrees."[48] Latitude indeed for a predestinarian!

Second, the inference attributes the belief in predestination exclusively to Calvinists, which cuts off Calvin rather rudely from centuries of tradition. The doctrine belongs to Christianity, and has done so ever since St. Paul. For example, the sardonic lines of Robert Burns—

> O thou, who in the heaven does dwell
> Who, as it pleases but Thysel,
> Sends ane to heaven an' ten to hell
> A' for thy glory,
> And no for any gude or ill
> They've done afore Thee[49]

—which were meant to represent the "Calvinist" view at its most inflexible, were anticipated by St. Augustine in *Enchiridion.* He,

too, stressed the double decree: "After the resurrection . . .
boundary lines will be set for the two cities: the one of Christ,
the other of the devil. . . . It is quite vain, then, that some—
indeed very many—yield to merely human feelings and deplore
the notion of eternal punishment of the damned."[50] "The eternal death of the damned—that is, their estrangement from the
life of God—will therefore abide without end, and it will be
common to them all, no matter what some people, moved by
their human feelings, may wish to think."[51] On this evidence
Whitgift could be called a Catholic, or, perhaps, a Lollard or a
Zwinglian. Moreover, a century after Calvin, Jansenism was
equally harsh. The last two books of the third volume of Jansen's
Augustinus (1640) develop the extreme notion appropriated to
Calvin. Yet agreement on the point did not prevent Jansen from
denouncing the great Calvinist controversialist Gisbert Voet, a
fact that suggests the secondary nature of the doctrine.[52] We do
not consider the pilgrim who fled toward the wicket gate crying
"Life, Life, Eternal Life!" a figure in the imagination of a Calvinist thinker.[53] We cannot claim that Separatists were really
Calvinists simply because they agreed on one particular doctrine. Double predestination was not a Calvinist monopoly.

The third flaw need only be stated: the judgment implies that
acceptance of one tenet involved belief in all.

An exaggerated emphasis on the doctrine of predestination
has warped our understanding of religious history, yet the warp
itself was a product of the past. Post-Restoration defenders of
Anglicanism found the extreme form of predestination called
as much for ridicule as for sober philosophic condemnation. It
was a handy stick with which to beat the Puritan dogs, as Samuel
Butler found in *Hudibras*. (Ben Jonson's satire of the sin-chop-
ping Puritan, Zeal-of-the-land Busy, in *Bartholomew Fair* may
have been the model for *Hudibras*.) At another level, Joseph
Glanvill attacked predestination in the "Antifanatick theologie"
of his *Essays*. The distortions of the past have become codified
in the present, possibly because predestination has seemed the
simplest interpretive key for unlocking the values and ethos of
Puritanism. Ernst Troeltsch and Max Weber fixed upon it as

the source of the "worldly asceticism" that seemed to characterize Calvinism in general,[54] and their choice was confirmed in
R. H. Tawney's masterpiece.[55] In deference to these colossi, subsequent historians have traced the same pattern. Indeed, so imposing is the list of scholars who stress predestination that their
collective judgment approaches dogma itself. It has become an
accepted presupposition of Puritan studies. William Haller, for
instance, called predestination "the central dogma of Puritanism," and suggested that "the history of Puritan thought in
England is primarily the history of the setting forth of the basic
doctrine of predestination in terms calculated to appeal to the
English populace."[56] The importance of the concept is a historians' myth that has worked its way as deeply as a linguistic
impurity into our thinking; it has been a beam obstructing our
sight of the antipathetic doctrinal assumptions.

A belief in man's total depravity heightened the awful sovereignty of God. Luther had contrasted man's sin with God's
love to establish the righteousness of God (*coram Deo*); Puritanism drew a similar contrast between man's sin and God's justice to magnify the glory of God (*gloria Deo*). The sharp an-
tinomy between man's abject predicament and God's immea-
surable power gave Puritanism its distinctive character, and lay
at the center of Puritan motivation. Only after we stop explaining Puritan behavior in terms of the merely derivative doctrine
of predestination, and link it to the central premises, can we
remedy some of the injustices of the accepted interpretation; for
by doing so, we reverse Napoleon's aphorism and turn Puritan
motives from the ridiculous to the sublime.[57] We find that every
action, instead of deriving from arrogant confidence in an abhorrent doctrine, sprang from a belief that even the smallest
trifle was part of a cosmic drama and pertinent to God's infinite
integrity.

Puritans were always giving God the glory. The purpose of
life, according to the Westminster Shorter Catechism, was to
worship God and glorify Him forever. So, at the moment of
victory at the Battle of Dunbar, Cromwell called his cavalry together to chant the 117th Psalm:

> O give ye praise unto the Lord
> All Nations that be.
> Likewise ye people all accord
> His name to magnify.[58]

Admittedly this was a tactical rally, but it was also a mark of faith. John Downame believed that the whole end of the Christian struggle against temptation was to exalt God's omnipotence. "But here it may be demanded, why the Lord will suffer his servants to be thus tempted and assaulted, whereas the wicked are free from such conflicts. I answer, first for his own glory, for whereas our enemies are strong and mighty and we weak and feeble, hereby is the Lord's omnipotent power manifested to all the world. . . . Secondly, God suffereth his children to be tempted, that so those spiritual graces which he hath bestowed upon them may the more clearly shine to his glory."[59] In the Puritans' sensitive, at times supersensitive, awareness of God's sovereignty, all things had to be subsumed to His glory.

This sensitivity to God's honor and power braced the Puritans' certainty about assurance; for if faith was granted by the Absolute Will, how could a believer fail or falter? Cartwright, in his Commentary on Colossians, stressed this point again and again. "We learn that they that are truly reconciled and called shall abide forever.—This is a true doctrine, a saint once, a saint forever.—It is impossible that they which believe should perish.— That as in Matthew the house founded on the rock can not be overthrown, Matt. vii. 24, so they that are grounded on Christ by Faith, Matt. xvi. 18, the very gates of hell shall not prevail against them."[60] Since God was unchanging, the knowledge of His assurance was unshakable. Circuitously, by way of the elevation of God's majesty, the notion of human worthlessness led to an intensified conviction of individual regeneracy. God could give man new dignity for old degeneracy.

Anglicanism was not so confident of assurance. We have already noticed the English Arminians, who affirmed that a man might renounce his saving inheritance. Assurance was contingent upon perseverance in faith. John Donne, who claimed in his *Sermons* to have little taste for quibbling about these problems, may be taken as typical.[61] "Consider how dangerously an abuse of the great doctrine of Predestination may bring thee to think, that God is bound to thee, and thou not bound to him, that thou mayest renounce him, and he must embrace thee, and so to make thee too familiar with God, and too homely with Religion, upon presumption of a Decree."[62] A lack of certainty lingers in Donne's reverence. And Hooker, too, can be considered representative because he spanned both Andrewes and Whitgift on the doctrine of predestination. As the Puritan Walter Travers complained, Hooker taught "that the assurance of that we believe by the word is not so certain as of that we perceive by the sense."[63] Travers' refutation confirms the distinction drawn here: Travers preached "the doctrine otherwise, namely, the assurance of faith to be greater, which assured both of things above and contrary to all sense and human understanding."[64] It was the Anglicans' attachment to reason and understanding—in other words, their view of man—that lessened their certainty about assurance of faith.

Anglican rationalism also tended to diminish the overriding importance of the sovereignty of God. The mere assertion of natural rationality closed the gap between God and man, so that God became less awesome. Thus Hooker could consider nature and grace contiguous extensions of God's purpose. Or, to draw support from evidence usually used in another connection, it is well known that Whitgift adopted a relativistic position against Cartwright on Church polity. "But that any one kind of government is so necessary that it may not be altered into some other kind thought to be more expedient I utterly deny."[65] Once the question had been removed from the context of salvation, considerations of expediency could come into play; and Whitgift found that present exigency was as pressing as apostolic example.[66] The truism that Anglicans were not slavish imitators of God's Word holds firm, but implies rather more than it says. It contains ideological implications at two levels: man's ability to reason made his earthly designs both plausible and commendable; and, at the same time, that very ability could limit the all-pervadingness of God's authority in the Scriptures.

These conceptions of man and his relationship to the Creator determined the standards of morality laid down by Anglicans and Puritans. Since ethics are the subject of Chapter 4, only personal standards will be considered now, those prescribed for society in general being dealt with later. Though the differences between the Anglican and Puritan views tend to attract all our attention, we should not overlook the areas of morality that were held in common. The vices of interest to the Dedham Classis in the 1580's, or the "scandals" listed by the Westminster Assembly as meriting exclusion from the sacrament, were one of a piece with Archbishop Laud's visitation articles to the diocese of St. David's.[67] Adulterers, fornicators, and those who had committed incest or incited women to unchastity; drunkards, blasphemers, swearers, slanderers, sowers of discord, filthy and lascivious talkers, usurers, and simonists; bawds and harborers of unmarried women with child; those using enchantments, sorcery, incantations, or witchcraft; perjurers, forgers and their procurers, and abettors—all were to be named for censure. The list does not turn Laud into a Puritan: his visitation articles were duplicates of earlier Anglican documents.[68] These categories— give or take a sin—were common to both parties, who read them as a roll call of wickedness.

Yet, despite the agreement, the marginal variations became the loci of irritation. Anglicanism, as we shall see, nursed in some a pietistic ethic that derived in part from uncertainty about assurance. Another obvious cause of friction was the fact that Anglicans saw no harm in worldly pleasures. Bodily adornment, dancing, Sunday sports, stage plays, and the like were regarded as perfectly seemly. John Donne thought the limits of beautifying one's body were not so narrow as "some sowre men" conceived them to be.[69] James I, in his *Book of Sports* (1618), berated those "precise persons" who claimed that enjoyment and recreation were incompatible with true religion. He recommended "that after the end of Divine Service, our good people be not disturbed, letted, or discouraged from any lawful Recreation; such as dancing, either men or women, Archery for men, leaping, vaulting, or any such harmless Recreation, nor from having of May-Games, Whitson-Ales, and Morris-Dances, and the setting up of May-poles and other sports therewith used." Charles I reissued his father's *Book of Sports* in 1633.

Such latitude was anathema to Puritans. Lucy Hutchinson, wife of the Puritan regicide John Hutchinson, was outraged because the people enjoyed "masks, stage-plays, and sorts of ruder sports."[70] William Prynne, in the Epistle Dedicatory to his massive *Histriomastix* (1632), could not say enough about the evils of the stage: "What profit do we reap from stage plays? Do they not enrage the lusts, add fire and fuel to [people's] unchaste affections, deprave their minds, corrupt their manners, cauterize their consciences, obdurate their heads, multiply their heinous transgressions, consume their estates, misspend their time, canker their graces, blast all their virtues, interrupt their studies, indispose them to repentance and true godly sorrow for their sins?" The Puritans were zealous to guard God's honor, swift and terrible to punish His dishonor. Tawney's vignette of their character will never be surpassed.[71] Those unrelenting moral Spartans had their sense of obligation augmented by a profound notion of sin, and they knew that God's assurance reinforced their collapsible resolve.[72] On the other hand, the Anglicans' sense of their own good sense allowed them to indulge in occasional whims and innocent pleasures.

The same construction of certainties—man's bottomless sin, God's sovereignty, and God's assurance—inspired Puritan activism. The Puritans' determination to reform the world, and their persistent urge to build the new Jerusalem, are well-known. John Milton, at this point still an Independent, never felt more optimistic than in the Civil War: England was called, that out of her as out of Zion should sound forth the "trumpet of Reformation to all Europe." "God is decreeing some new and great period in his Church, ev'n to the reforming of Reformation itself."[73] Travers' solemn promise to observe "the Public Laws of the Kingdom and . . . the Peace of the church" had little chance of being fulfilled, for he was compelled to agitation.[74] Worldly pleasure, preferment, and court office, even life itself, were sacrificed for religious conviction. The dedication of Puritans overflowed. "Let Christ Jesus be your all in all," wrote one who was deprived of the stumps of his ears for conscience's sake, "your only solace, your only Spectacle, and joy on earth, whose soul-ravishing heart-filling presence, shall be your eternal solace, your everlasting all-glorious most triumphant Spectacle in the highest heaven."[75] The Separatists' cry of "Reformation without tarrying for any" captures the Puritan ethos in a phrase.[76] The Puritans' extraordinary energy could not have been generated by the more flexible conscience of Anglicanism; it was unleashed by the absolute conviction that there was no good in man until he had learned to conform with God's revealed intentions.

Anglicans were not less dedicated, but their aims were conservative: they were in love with the *status quo*. To say that makes them neither black reactionaries nor obstinate opponents of gradual improvement. Their kind of conservatism stemmed from the assumption that man-made edifices could be, and in this case were, satisfactory. Changes, therefore, ought to be carefully deliberated with an eye on the possible future consequences. Precisely this feeling permeated Whitgift's and Hookers' apologias. Their forebodings painfully anticipated the immediate and distant repercussions of Puritan demands—and, as it turned out, with foresight.[77] The Puritans' clamor would bring about the collapse of the Church and reduce it to impotent fragments. The clergy would fall into disrespect. Factional differences would undermine the zeal for proper worship and true piety. Moreover, the Puritan obsession with change would affect not only the Church but also the body politic. The Queen's prerogative would be undermined; all social order, legal principles, and university education would be thrown into disarray. The whole nation would tumble headlong into confusion, and the intricate fabric of English society would be rent apart.

It may seem that such extravagant prognostications could have been voiced only by arch-defenders of the Establishment. But even Ussher, a monument of clerical mildness, warned the Puritans of the dangers ahead: "The beginning of contention thou thinkest is but a small matter; why, so it is but a small matter to open a dam. . . . Therefore leave it off now, it lies in your power to stop it. A child may be able to [set] fire [to] an house, but it will trouble and pose the wits of a thousand to quench it again when it hath gotten head. Now to what end is all this? . . . We see the ruins of the Kingdom, the destruction of the state and church."[78] Anglicanism was pessimistic about reform, yet it is no twist of logic to see the cause of its pessimism in optimism about human nature. If man was skilled enough to build a goodly church, then any hasty renovation, any ill-conceived addition, could do irreparable damage to the present pleasing structure.

Different views about man's innate capacity led to different patterns of thought as a whole. The fact that Anglicans, from Cranmer to Laud, shared a faith in the natural reason remaining to man, even after the Fall, places Hooker in an indigenous tradition without detracting from his originality. Style apart, his genius was to bring the common assumption to the surface, and to offer it explicitly as the cosmic basis of the Church Establishment. Our concern is not with Hooker's thought *per se,* but with the doctrinal preconditions it illuminates.[79] First, Hooker's rationality was communal: he assumed that reason was diffused, in varying degrees, throughout the whole community. Second, it was traditional: past society had entrusted valuable depositions to the present. Third, reason was contiguous to grace: law emanated from "the bosom of God" in a harmonious chain; and the gradations of law, though integral parts of this Divine chain or stairway, were separate from each other, so that men were not angels nor animals men. Fourth, reason was divine, since God was its author. And finally, though it carry men far, reason was of limited power. Divine efficiency was far beyond it, and divine dispensations came by revelation alone.

Subsequent thinkers elaborated various aspects of Hooker's *Polity.* Edmund Burke revered "the wisdom of the nation" that valued its inheritance from the past. John Locke utilized the concept of men bound by the law of Nature. Thomas Hobbes, after describing an intolerable state of nature, trusted to the universal human desire for felicity to bring society together under an absolute authority. He expected too much of reason rather than too little. Natural reason was a malleable instrument and could be bent to many purposes. Political philosophers may have turned Hooker's concepts from a heavenly to an earthly usage, but the Cambridge Platonists accurately reflected his notion of the spirituality of reason. "The spirit of man is the candle of the Lord" was Whichcote's favorite text.[80] That Hooker sired such diverse progeny shows the strength of his reputation as a seminal figure in the Church. Anglicanism was indebted to Hooker, and Hooker to Anglicanism; for the Church's doctrine was the platform from which he projected his urbane rationality—a rationality grounded on the wisdom within the community at large.

A divergence between Christians who would wed wisdom to revelation and those who sharply distinguished the spheres of knowledge is as old as the second-century Greek and Latin apologists. Justin Martyr had contended that Christian revelation was the consummation of Greek philosophy, whereas Tertullian, like St. Paul, claimed that secular philosophy was a snare for seekers after truth. Or, in the twelfth century, the Scholastic Peter Abélard and the mystic St. Bernard of Clairvaux illustrate the opposite poles. The divergence is also as modern as Karl Barth's reaction to liberal theology. Christianity has long battled within the range of the two extremes: between secular reasoning as consubstantial with faith or as inimical to it.

Puritanism did not scorn knowledge as such, or even regard it as irrelevant to God, but it was wholly irrelevant to salvation, and any glorying in it was a cardinal sin. Thus Puritanism relied on the Scriptures, and the Scriptures alone, as its guide for good behavior. Cartwright's celebrated attacks on Whitgift epitomize the Puritan outlook: Whitgift would "take up and shrink the arms of the scripture which otherwise are so long and large."[81] Or he would injure the Word of God "to pin it in so narrow room, as that it should be able to direct us but in the principal points of religion."[82] Cartwright was a Scriptural totalitarian. "I say the word of God containeth the direction of all things, pertaining to the Church, yea, of whatsoever things can fall into any part of a man's life."[83]

Later, Richard Baxter was still advocating the same absolute criterion. He prefaced *The Christian Directory* (1673), in effect an encyclopedia of theology and ethics, with the directive "He that will walk uprightly must have a certain, just, infallible rule; and must hold to that, and try all by it; and this is only the Word of God."[84] And in *The Saints' Everlasting Rest* (1650) he begged his readers to "love, reverence, read, study, obey and stick close to the Scripture," the only sure yardstick of human behavior.[85] "Neither the learned, nor the godly, nor the good must be our rule," but Scripture alone.[86] In theory, Puritans relied upon the Word of God for every decision of daily living. Since they considered man too wretched to discipline himself, they had no choice but to impose this monolithic standard upon themselves.

Obviously the Scriptures are susceptible of a wide variety of interpretation. So, very naturally, historians have assumed that Puritanism's fixation upon the Word was the source of its individualism and its tendency to fragmentation. This may be, but I am inclined to believe that other factors were at work, notably the doctrine of the Church and the metaphysical theory behind it, and that the Scriptural glosses of various groups were made in concert with these other, perhaps deeper, assumptions. The Puritans' reliance on the Scriptures hid a rationalism of a subjective kind. When Travers criticized Hooker for referring too readily to rational authority, Hooker patiently explained that he was quoting the authorities not to add weight to the Scriptures, but to try to clarify some of the obscurer meanings of the Holy Writ. Travers, he countered, used the same technique without admitting it; neither did he cite corroborating opinion, but followed his own wit and will under the pretense of spiritual discernment.[87] How irritating those two must have found each other! Puritanism's subjective rationality was not, of course, confined to the pulpit: it flooded into politics and other fields. For example, Cromwell's justifications by Divine Providence were no more than sanctifications for personal success, as one of his critics pointed out: "To say that he hath [power] by Providence;

that argument is but like a two edged sword, and a thief may lay as good a title to every purse he takes upon the highway."[88] Cromwell's notion of calling was as brittle a theory of Divine Right as King Charles's had ever been. In sum, Puritan behavior, as much as Anglican, had its own peculiar rationalism: the one was the device of the self-disciplined conscience; the other contrived to mirror the consensus of society.

In this context, to describe the Puritan-Anglican struggles as a collision of conscience against conformity is superficial. Equally, the contrast between Scripturalism and traditionalism is unwarranted; for if the Elizabethan Settlement retained some of the old outward forms, it broke decisively with the past doctrinally, and the forms were but the veneer, the doctrines the substance. Furthermore, Anglicanism was profoundly Scriptural. Much to the Puritans' chagrin, the Anglicans eventually discovered Scriptural proof for episcopacy, so the debate in the seventeenth century could be described as being between Scripturalists and Scripturalists.[89]

In reality the antagonisms arose from two incompatible habits of Biblical exegesis, each consistent with its own rationality. Puritanism claimed that Scripture revealed the model for Church organization, and for all behavior; that what was in Scripture ought to be implemented, and what was not explicitly there ought not to be practiced. Anglicanism considered the Scriptures authoritative for all things that pertained to redemption, but permissive for those that did not, in which case men might adjust their own affairs.[90]

This dispute about the authority of Scripture is generally accepted as the critical point of a long controversy, but clearly the point was determined by the intersection of two differing concepts of human nature. For Anglicanism, man was at once a miserable sinner and, within worldly limits, a rational creature. Puritan dogma held man to be fallen in every faculty and utterly depraved. The overlap with Anglicans on the doctrine of predestination should not blind us to the possibility of far-reaching doctrinal differences on other issues. In fact, such differences existed, and were fundamental: Puritanism's sense of obligation and assurance, and its morality, activism, exegetical habit, and total rationality, derived from one view of human nature, whereas the relative uncertainty of the Anglicans' assurance, and their temperance, conservatism, patristic interpretation of Scripture, and communal rationalism, stemmed from another. And in turn the alien concepts of man were determined by an apparently slight disagreement in the measurement of his alienation from God.

Chapter 2 The Church

Anglicans and Puritans shared the idea of the Church as a dispensary of the means of grace. Grace, perhaps, is one of the most eloquent and complex of theological words, but here it is intended very simply and broadly to mean God's sanctifying activity. In Troeltsch's terminology, both Anglicanism and Puritanism presupposed a "church-type" Church. That is to say, they regarded the Church as an institution "endowed with grace and salvation as the result of the redemption."[1] Yet Troeltsch's distinction between church-type and sect-type Christianity cannot be perfectly sustained in this case because Anglicanism contained elements of mysticism, and Puritanism an enthusiastic impulse toward congregationalism, both of which were sect-type tendencies. Neither group, however, thought of the Church as a voluntary gathering of true believers who lived in imitation of Christ and expected His return at any minute. They were not Sectaries. Rather, the Church was designed to be all-inclusive, and consequently it tended to be worldly, as it could afford to be because of the quality and monopoly of the spiritual goods it distributed. Troeltsch's church-type category is a capacious one: Roman Catholicism belongs to it as much as Anglicanism and Puritanism.* So once again we should stress that we are dealing with disparities between groups that held much in common, including the urge to remain, or become, institutionalized, and to enfold the whole of society to the Church's bosom.

This agreement implies that both Anglicans and Puritans

---

* All Protestantism denied the claim of the Pope to supervise affairs of the soul. Anglicanism regarded Papal infallibility and the pretension to hold the Keys as utterly unfounded and idolatrous. Over a century this positive rejection did not weaken or waver. Laud's arguments were replicas of John Jewel's. Anglicanism was as Protestant as Puritanism on this score. See, e.g., Laud, *Works*, II, 3–21, and Jewel, *Works*, IV, 1035–37; Laud, *Works*, II, 231, 297, and Jewel, *Works*, I, 401, IV, 925.

wanted to preserve the traditional conjunction of Church and State. A national *corpus Christianum,* or Christian realm, was their common ideal. Hooker hoped that "there is not any man of the Church of England but the same is also a member of the Commonwealth, nor any man a member of the Commonwealth, which is not also of the Church of England."[2] Puritanism, as much as Anglicanism, desired a Church joined to the State—though with somewhat changed relationships. For example, in 1645, under pressure from the Scots, the Presbyterian majority of the Long Parliament imposed on England and Wales a Directory for Public Worship, in testimony, they declared, of their godly "endeavours for Uniformity."[3] Cromwell later labored to replace this institution with a loosely organized system of Independency; and he was outraged by the maneuvers of those Fifth Monarchist disestablishmentarians whom he had mistaken for friends. The Army Debate at Whitehall (December 1648) made it plain that Independents would have no truck with Separatism, though they were prepared to tolerate the Sectaries so long as they behaved themselves.[4]

Thus the body of agreement was considerable: both parties wanted a Church that commanded objective means of grace under Christ, that was institutionalized and comprehensive, and that was joined to the State. In addition, both maintained intercommunion with the same foreign Churches; and both categorically denied the Papal supremacy. All these were substantial bonds, yet the agreements themselves contributed to internecine disagreement. This was inevitable; for given incompatible assumptions but identical aims, a fierce struggle for power was bound to occur. So long as the two groups' aims for the Church coincided, a lasting peace was possible only after one group had defeated or, to use Milton's word, church-outed the other.

Historiographically, however, the broad measures of agreement have been thrown in apposition to the points of disagreement, with the result that at and after the Settlement the practical differences appear to be extremely slight. Indeed the contrast makes rather a riddle out of the whole Anglican-Puritan conflict. Consequently historians have long pondered why churchmen who agreed in so much should fall at odds, and the explanations have been remarkably uniform. Yet a uniformity of learned judgment is no guarantee of truth; we may have been misled by the Bellman's principle in *The Hunting of the Snark,* "What I tell you three times is true." Repetition may have convinced us that the differences were organizational, Calvinistic forms against Episcopalian uses. Thomas Fuller's *Church History,* written during the Civil Wars and Interregnum—the heyday of constitutional experimentation—told of the changes and controversies in Church affairs with such sweet and witty moderation that it is difficult to bear in mind the bitterness of the quarrel. The historians' orientation toward Church government began then and has not changed substantially since. A century and a half later, Daniel Neal foreshadowed the Whig orthodoxy by arguing that the conflicts, petty enough to start with, were precipitated, and later grossly extended, by clerical intolerance and severity.[5] In other words, the Puritans were really fighting for toleration, though too often they betrayed their historic mission when they were in power.

After judicious devaluation, Neal's analysis has remained negotiable currency. Among modern writers, W. K. Jordan (following Milton's line of argument) discovered that the Presbyterians were far from tolerant, but the Separatists eminently so.[6] The contemporaries' charge that Puritanism threatened the royal supremacy, since it was borne out by the events, has remained a primary component in our interpretation. Similarly, Troeltsch's conclusions about Continental Calvinism have never been seriously questioned. He attributed Calvinistic individualism and the "holy community" character of the Calvinist Church to the commitments that predestination imposed upon the believer and to single-minded Scripturalism. "This idea of a 'holy community' . . . springs out of the same principle which appears to give independence to the individual, namely, out of the ethical duty of the preservation and making effective of election, and out of the abstract exaltation of the Scriptures."[7] His interpretation has been reaffirmed by Haller, M. M. Knappen, and a legion of others.

But is this view entirely correct? The last chapter tried to reduce the oversize proportions of double predestination, and cautioned against giving Scripturalism an exclusively Puritan billing. The Puritans' use of the Scriptures was but one aspect of a total rationale deriving from their pessimistic view of human nature in general. In a similar way, this chapter will try to relate the tensions between the Anglican and the Puritan forms of churchmanship to each group's underlying doctrinal preconceptions.

A "holy community" character did indeed color Puritan Church practice, and it was also a mark of Puritanism's proximity to voluntaryism and Separatism. Rather than predestinarianism or Scripturalism, however, a dogmatic annulment of the distinction between the visible and the invisible Church explains this quality in Puritan churchmanship. Perhaps because Troeltsch did not mention it, the merger has passed unnoticed in the prevailing explanations, yet it would appear to be a touchstone of Church practice.

In the abstract, Calvin had recognized the two kinds of Churches, but he proceeded to nullify the difference by blandly equating the external Church with the spiritual society. "We are not enjoined here to distinguish between the elect and the reprobate (this belongs not to us but to God alone) but to feel firmly assured in our minds, that all those who, by the mercy of God the Father, through the efficacy of the Holy Spirit, have become partakers with Christ, are set apart as the proper and peculiar possession of God, and that as we are of this number, we are also partakers of His great grace."[8] Thus for practical purposes the visible was assumed to be the invisible Church.

Similarly, in John Cotton's *The Way of the Churches of Christ in New England* (1645), one can see not only this merging of the visible and invisible Church, but also the urge to voluntaryism that it encouraged. According to Cotton, Church policy on admission was that "though we willingly admit all comers to the hearing of the word with us . . . yet we receive none as members into the church but such as (according to the judgement of Charitable Christians) may be conceived to be received into the

fellowship with Christ, the head of the church. . . . Nevertheless, in this trial, we do not exact eminent measure, either of
knowledge or holiness, but do willingly stretch out our hands
to receive the weak in faith, such in whose spirits we can discern
the least measure of panting after Christ, in their sensible feeling
of a lost estate."[9] Cotton favored a comprehensive Church, and
yet at the same time, like Calvin, regarded all members as "partakers with Christ" and "set apart" in His "proper and peculiar
possession." He assumed that the Church visible was the holy
community; but unlike Calvin he carried the identification to
the brink of Separatism. Plainly, in practice, any attempt to draw
the two kinds of Churches together involved exclusiveness and
tended to voluntaryism. In this sense, voluntaryism was inherent
in the Puritans' Church dogma.

That the visible Church could be thought of as spiritual was
partly due to Puritanism's theory of regenerate man. By nature
man was utterly depraved; in the church, however, under the
impressions of grace, the truly converted received a new nature
—or a partially restored nature—that left him open to temptation but ensured his final perseverance. There was, as William
Ames explained in *The Marrow of Sacred Divinity* (1638?),
"an alteration of qualities made in man himself," "a real change
of a man from the filthiness of sin, to the purity of God's
image."[10] The Puritans' insistence upon the work of grace in the
believer further strengthened their resolve and assurance (as
already discussed). In addition, the genuine conversion, with its
subjective assurance, placed the believer somewhat apart from
the sinner, and hence, collectively, insulated the Church in the
minds of churchmen from the world.

The Puritans' conception of the relationship between grace
and nature also infused spirituality into the visible Church.*
Puritanism rejected grace as a gift added to nature, a spiritual
complement to intellect; instead, grace stood in a dialectical
relationship to nature, incommensurate and yet concurrent.
This metaphysical theory had been systematically developed by

---

* Nature is used in this chapter to mean human nature and not the physical universe.

Calvin. The incommensurability of the two spheres is the main argument of his *Commentaries on Genesis*: "It is vain for any to reason as philosophers on the workmanship of the world, except those who, having been humbled by the preaching of the Gospel, have learned to submit the whole of their intellectual wisdom (as Paul expresses it) to the foolishness of the cross (I Cor. i. 21)."[11] Grace was outside and beyond the dimensions of nature, a theme pursued by John Owen in the *Exposition of Psalm CXXX*: "Forgiveness . . . is not a property of the nature of God, but an act of his will, and a work of his grace. . . . There is no inbred notion of the acts of God's will in the hearts of men. . . . Forgiveness is not revealed by the light of nature. Flesh and blood, which nature is, reveal it not."[12] At the same time, Calvin saw these incomparable essences as working together: grace was continually confronting man, and man, when converted, was not merely improved but radically changed and renewed. "After Adam had by his own desperate fall viewed himself and all his posterity, this is the basis of our salvation, this is the origin of the church, that we, being rescued out of profound darkness, have obtained new life by the mere grace of God."[13]

Grace was locked in a dialectical tension with nature. Like St. Augustine, Richard Baxter interpreted human history as the epic of God's struggle with Satan for men's souls. And Owen's work *Of Sin and Grace* claimed that "the sensible powerful actings of indwelling sin are not inconsistent with a state of grace, Gal. v. 17. There are in the same persons contrary principles, 'the flesh against the Spirit,' these are contrary: and there are contrary actings from these principles; 'the flesh lusteth against the Spirit, and the Spirit against the flesh.'"[14] Similarly, Perkins held that "the Grace of God for the time of this life is mixed with his contrary, the corruption of the flesh."[15] He went on: "In nature we cannot pass from one contrary to the other, but by the mixture of contraries: as in light and darkness, the one doth not follow the other immediately; but first, there is a mixture of them both in the dawning of the day, and closing of the night: and so it is in other contraries, even those which concern the soul: unbelief is sin, faith is a virtue and grace contrary to it. Now unbelief cannot be expelled by faith, before there be a mixture of them both, and so when faith prevaileth, unbelief decayeth: neither can faith ever be perfect, because it is ever mingled more or less with unbelief."[16] It was, according to Adams, the ministers' function to reconcile the "two contrary natures, sinfull men, and Righteousness" within their flocks.[17]

Puritanism was, of course, being scrupulously consistent with its extreme view of human corruption to place grace in flat contradiction to nature. Thus, metaphysically, grace was separated from nature. Yet grace was also associated with nature, not in an echelon relationship, but as a substance surrounding and diffused through the nature of every sanctified person. Perhaps the interrelationships between the two spheres can be best described as a dialectical juxtaposition. This non-hierarchical metaphysical theory allowed Puritanism to equate the visible with the spiritual Church. On the one hand Puritanism believed that the Church stored the means of grace, and on the other it recognized that all men were perverse, even the saved. Since, however, grace coexisted with its contrary, human depravity could be maintained and the contradictions resolved by assuming that the Church had been suffused by God's sanctifying Spirit.

Anglicanism, in contrast, retained the traditional dichotomy between the visible and the invisible Church, a principle manifest in Whitgift's famous dispute with Cartwright. "There are two kinds of government in the church, the one invisible, the other visible: the one spiritual, the other eternal. The invisible and spiritual government of the church is, when God by his spirit, gifts and ministering of his Word, doth govern it, by ruling in the hearts and conscience of men, and directing them in all things necessary to everlasting life: this kind of government, indeed, is necessary to salvation, and it is the church of the elect only. The visible and external government is that which is executed by man, and consisteth in external discipline, and visible ceremonies practised in the church and over the church, that maintaineth in it both 'good and evil,' which is usually called the visible church of Christ, and compared by Christ to 'a field' wherever both 'good seeds' and 'tares were sown' and to 'a net that gathered all kinds of fishes.' "[18] Whitgift distinguished the two so sharply in order to counter the Puritan's opposite trend.

Having set the Establishment squarely in the realm of nature, Anglicans could believe that the ceremonies, order of worship, discipline, and form of government of the Church were matters properly determined by experience, convenience, and reason.[19] That these considerations formed the crux of the Elizabethan controversy about the Church has been extensively argued and assiduously documented. One explanation emphasizes Anglican subservience to the Crown, which, to be sure, was a powerful attitude, but not a controlling one: it can scarcely be attributed to those who fled Mary's accession; and it is hard to believe that it dominated men who remembered the Marian martyrs. Another suggestion, "traditionalism," has little meaning when it is made to blanket the whole issue: clearly, it does not apply to self-acknowledged Protestants, some of whom had helped to frame, and all of whom defended, the recently established doctrine; and to explain the behavior of those who wanted to retain the old forms by an unspecific traditionalism borders on tautology. Finally, there is the political explanation that the Anglicans' care to preserve outward continuity was imperative if they wanted to achieve their goals of a peaceful Settlement and a comprehensive Church—an attractive theory until we remember that these were the goals of the Puritans, too. Perhaps Anglicans were congenitally conservative and Puritans radical, which would support Gilbert's theory in *Iolanthe* (Act II)

> That every boy and every gal
> That's born unto the world alive
> Is either a little lib-er-al
> Or else a little con-ser-vat-ive.

Certainly Anglicanism nourished a conservatism based on its trust in man's natural ability; even so, the Church need not have been fixed so rigidly in the realm of nature.

The behavior of the Marian exiles abroad offers us insight into Anglican motives, for it is something like a control test. All the exiles were recent Protestants, yet some adopted the standards of Geneva while others retained their Anglican manners. The groups at Strasbourg and Zurich staunchly defended Cranmer's revised Prayer Book against a Genevan substitute, and one suspects that more than mere obstinacy was involved. At Frankfurt, Richard Chambers and Edmund Grindal had urged, and Richard Cox implemented, concession to the local environment by dropping private baptism, confirmation, saints' days, kneeling to receive, the surplice, crosses, and the like. There were considerable concessions, and it is hard to reconcile Anglican conservatism with such ready pliability. Anglican rationalism, however, which respected the communal wisdom of a society, fits the cases both at home and abroad. On another occasion, the Anglicans at Frankfurt, apparently so pliable on some matters, fought bitterly with the Calvinists over whether an English or a Genevan form should be used by the congregation. Similarly, the Anglican Richard Horne waged a bitter battle to maintain clerical control of the congregation. Nowadays the struggles read like comic melodramas tinged with tragedy.[20] Historically, the factors usually advanced as the causes of contention had no relevance whatever in the situation—subservience, outward traditionalism, or polite efforts to maintain a comprehensive Church. Therefore, unless we are to regard the exiles as incorrigibly capricious —conciliatory at one moment, cantankerous at the next—we must assume that religious convictions were at stake, in particular, contrary notions of the true nature of the Church.

As with the Puritans, metaphysical presuppositions were embedded in the Anglicans' view of the Church. Their understanding of the relationships between the spheres of grace and nature proscribed any mistaking of the visible for the invisible society. They were forced to emphasize the visible Church because they regarded grace as being arranged in a tiered relationship with nature: the two spheres belonged to two levels. Grindal's discussion of the sacrament makes this clear: "And whereas I say that Christ's body must be received and taken with faith I mean not that you shall pluck down Christ from heaven and put him in your faith, as in a visible place; but that you must with your faith run and spring up to him, and leaving this world, dwell above in heaven."[21]

Richard Field's universe, too, like Hooker's and Shakespeare's, was hierarchically ordered: "All other things seek no higher perfection nor greater good than is found within the compass of their own nature . . . but men and Angels which seek an infinite and Divine good, even the everlasting and endless happiness, which consisteth in the vision of God . . . cannot attain the wished good; which is so high and excellent, and so far removed from them, unless by supernatural force, which we call grace, they be lifted up unto it. For though by nature they know God, so far forth as by his efforts and glorious works he may be known; yet as he is himself they know him not, farther than in the light of grace and glory he is pleased to manifest himself unto them. . . . To this Angels may be lifted up, to this they cannot ascend themselves; to this man cannot go, to this he may be drawn. . . . Those things which are inferior unto man can neither attain by themselves, nor be drawn, nor lifted up to the partaking of this so happy and joyful estate."[22]

Finally, we have already noticed the contiguity of grace to nature in Hooker's thought. Although Hooker allowed reason a little more scope than Field, the metaphysical content of his thinking was the same: "For our conversion or confirmation the force of natural reason is great. [But] the force whereof unto those effects is nothing without grace."[23] According to this view, grace did not struggle with nature; it completed it: "Scripture teacheth things above nature, things which our reason itself could not reach unto."[24] Or again: "The operations of the Spirit . . . are as we know things secret and undiscernible even to the very soul where they are, because their nature is of another and an higher kind than that they can be by us perceived."[25]

Like the Puritans, though in a different way, the Anglicans isolated and associated the spheres of grace and nature. Grace could descend to elevate man, and nature could not of itself ascend to grace. The two realms were hierarchically rather than dialectically linked and differentiated.

Besides being a distributor of grace, the Church was, theoretically, an all-inclusive social institution. In view of this, the metaphysical conception of nature under grace had the effect of constraining the Church within the realm of nature; and, by confining the Church to nature, the Anglicans kept the way open for the use of "assimilative rationality" in deciding the Church's outward forms and polity. The metaphysical construction of grace above nature, and nature beneath grace, was therefore a fundamental part of Anglican traditionalism; for while it remained, the Church had to be thought of as belonging to nature. Whereas Puritan doctrine spiritualized the Church, Anglican doctrine, so to speak, visibilized it.

Combined with the basic Protestantism of Anglicanism, this placing of the Church in the realm of nature diluted the awareness of the communion of saints. Invocation of the saints was, of course, forbidden by the doctrine of justification by faith, which disallowed the imputation of any merit other than Christ's.[26] In accordance with the separation of the metaphysical spheres, Anglicans continued to regard the saints as existing above, but since supplication to them was prohibited, the spiritual stimulus that had been felt so strongly by Roman Catholics was lost. The movement away from Catholicism in this regard becomes evident if we compare the Prayer Book of 1549 with that of 1552. The former, in the communion order, prayed for the whole state of Christ's Church; the latter prayed specifically for the whole state of Christ's Church militant here on earth. In the communion service, Anglicans used the Nicene Creed, though the Apostles' Creed was recited at Morning Prayer. Puritans objected to the Nicene Creed, and advocated the exclusive use of the Apostles' Creed, ostensibly because it was of earlier origin (a second- instead of a fourth-century compilation). A more plausible explanation, however, may lie in the fact that the Nicene Creed omitted the phrase "the communion of saints," an omission that would have irritated Puritans.

Anglicanism not only lost much of Catholicism's feeling for the immanence of the saints, but was unable to replace it with Puritanism's idea of an intimate and ever-present communion: the fellowship of saints thus became an attribute of heaven rather than a reality that could be experienced in the fellowship of the visible Church.

The de-emphasis of this doctrine in turn diminished the communal enthusiasm in the Anglican service of worship. Although such an ethos was intangible, its loss bothered the Puritans considerably. The tone of established worship seemed unreal to them: divine service was unmoving and impersonal. The author of the Second Admonition to Parliament (1572) attacked the artificiality of the revised Prayer Book thus: "The Book is such a piece of work as it is strange we will use it, besides I cannot account it praying, as they use it commonly, but only reading or saying of prayers, even as a child that learned to read, if his lesson be a prayer, he doth not pray, even so it is commonly a saying, and reading prayers and not praying. . . . For though they have many guises, now to kneel, and now to stand, these be matters of course, and not any prick of conscience, or piercing of the heart . . . One he kneeleth on his knees, and this way he looketh and that way he looketh, another he kneeleth himself fast asleep, another he kneeleth with such devotion, that is so far in talk, that he forgetteth to arise till his knees ache, or his talk endeth, or the service is done! And why is all this? But that there is no such praying as should touch the heart."[27]

The charge of impersonality underlies the Puritans' distaste for rote responses, Scripture-reading without exposition, and the use of homilies for sermons, all of which, they claimed, reduced church worship to "base reading and service saying."[28] Their dislike of homilies was essentially a *cri de coeur* for the sermon to make a dramatic spiritual impact upon the worshipers. "We are lost; they cannot find us: we are sick; they cannot heal us: we are hungry; they cannot feed us, except they lead us by other men's lights, and heal us by saying a prescript form of service, or else feed us with homilies that are too homely to be set in place of God's Scripture."[29] The allusion was to *The Homily for Repairing and Keeping Clean of Churches*. Puritans wanted to be challenged by the sermon, edified by the Word, captivated in prayer.

According to the Puritans, the Anglican form of worship not

only lacked personal impact, but failed to involve the congregation as a whole: they wanted a stronger feeling of corporateness than Anglicanism offered. This may seem a curious conclusion, since the Liturgy was largely written in the first and second persons plural—at least an outward sign of corporateness—and the responses were a continuous invitation to the congregation to participate. The Puritan objection, however, was that the responses did not fulfill their function; they became mechanical reactions. Puritans did not want to jettison the Liturgy, but to perfect it. Some felt the intensity of congregational worship was hampered by "the skudding up and down of the minister from place to place, as to the chancel for saying the service and singing the communion, to the body of the church for the Litany and marriage, to the Church door for Baptism, and to the churchyard stile for burial."[30] Almost all of them were disturbed by the lack of spiritual fellowship in the communion service. John Field and Thomas Wilcox, the authors of the First Admonition (1572), urged that the sacrament should be delivered "generally and indefinitely, Take ye and eat ye," as it had been formerly, and not, as now, "particularly and singularly, Take thou and eat thou."[31] In reply Whitgift merely reaffirmed the very particularism they attacked: "Forasmuch as every one that receiveth this sacrament hath to apply unto himself the benefits of Christ's death and passion, therefore it is convenient to be said to every one, 'Take thou and eat thou.'"[32] This Anglican particularism in the sacraments—an outgrowth from basic doctrines—became increasingly marked.

After Charles I had adjudicated the altar controversy of the 1630's, and Laud had put his wishes into force, the practices that the Puritans most disliked became standard form. The Root and Branch Petition (1640) complained that some of the clergy would not move the table from the east end to the middle of the chancel for celebration.* They were therefore "forcing the people to come up thither to receive, or else denying the sacrament to them."[33] Communion, Puritans felt, had become a spec-

---

* In fact, if the table were railed in, they could not have moved it.

tacle, and the opportunity for congregational fellowship had been completely discarded. Puritanism fought this sacramental individualism tooth and nail by equating it with Romanism: private baptism and celebrating for a small number of communicants smacked of Popery; communion offered as a spectacle was designed to inspire idolatry. The Puritans' alacrity to detect errors, and their exaggerations, were responses to the mechanical nature and individualistic emphasis of Anglican worship.

Puritanism, because it presumed that the Church was suffused with grace and sanctity, retained a powerful sense of the communion of saints. The saints were those both of the past and of the present: those with God, and those on their way to God through pilgrimage on earth. Calvin, obviously aware that he was rehabilitating a forgotten doctrine, drew particular attention to this phrase of the Apostles' Creed in his *Institutes*:* "Hence the additional expression, the 'communion of saints,' for this clause, though usually omitted by ancient writers, must not be overlooked, as it admirably expresses the quality of the church; just as if it had been said, that the saints are united in the fellowship of Christ on this condition, that all the blessings which God bestows upon them are mutually communicable to each other."[34] Similarly, Richard Baxter, in that classic of English Puritanism *The Saints' Everlasting Rest,* spoke of looking forward to fellowship in heaven with "all the perfected spirits of the just," since he had already tasted penultimate bliss in the company of the saints on earth.[35] The idea of the Church as a gathering of visible saints was not only foreign to Anglicans, but feared by them. Their fears, moreover, were justified, for by way of an intensified congregationalism the Puritan emphasis could lead to Separatism.

Inevitably the stress on the communion of saints heightened the spiritual enthusiasm of the congregation. Baxter's parting advice to his parishioners at Kidderminster was to "be sure to maintain a constant delight in God, and a seriousness and spirit-

---

* Calvin's emphasis incidentally supports the suggestion that the Puritans' preference for the Apostles' Creed over the Nicene Creed was based, in part, on this small doctrinal point.

uality in all his worship."[36] Puritanism opposed spirituality of worship to Anglican formality, fellowship to the individualistic and mechanical performance of the service. Thus Church doctrine created the incongruous situation whereby Anglicans worshiped as a corporation of individuals, and Puritans as a community of congregations.

As we have noted, congregationalism linked Puritanism to Separatism. Within a church-type framework, Independency represented a rationalization of the congregational habit in a decentralized system of government. George Yule, in a thoughtful monograph, has suggested that the impetus for toleration came from Independency's demand for a decentralized form of Calvinist organization.[37] If the Church was to remain comprehensive, toleration would have to accompany decentralization as a matter of course. As it turned out under Cromwell, the Independent Establishment was both less and more than decentralized Calvinism. It was less in that Cromwell refused to allow Parliament to call an Assembly to draw up a body of doctrine, or to frame a liturgy for the Church; he would not allow even a list of damnable heresies to be drawn up. His Church therefore lacked defined doctrine, and, apart from the Commissions of Triers and Ejectors,* proper organs for enforcing discipline. This lack explains the popularity of the Worcester Association, an organization formed by Baxter in the 1650's to exercise Church discipline. The Settlement was more than decentralized Calvinism in that Cromwell was more tolerant than his classical Independent brethren, such as John Owen and Hugh Peter. He wanted the Church to be as broadly based as possible. Our concern, however, is less with the Interregnum Church Settlement than with the reasons why the Independents wanted more local autonomy for the parishes.

Underlying the obvious and unhelpful explanation that the Independents wanted a more thoroughgoing reformation than the Presbyterians are two related variations of emphasis. First, the Independents strengthened the "holy community" notion of

---

* These were two commissions set up by ordinances in 1654 to judge candidates for preaching positions and to evict existing ministers whom they considered unfit. The two commissions had jurisdiction in England and should be distinguished from a third commission, also set up in 1654, that tried ministers for benefices in Scotland.

the Church; and, second, they intensified the corporate ethos of the congregation. Perhaps the two are interdependent. In any event, the first catechism of Independency, Henry Jacobs' *Principles and Foundations of Christian Religion* (1604?), illustrates the quantitative differences:*

> Question. What is a true visible and Ministerial church of Christ?
> Answer. A true visible and Ministerial church of Christ is a particular congregation being a spiritual, perfect corporation of Believers and having power in it self immediately from church to administer all Religious means of faith to the members thereof.
> Question. How is a Visible Church constituted or gathered?
> Answer. By a free mutual consent of Believers joining and covenanting to live as Members of a holy Society together in all religious and virtuous duties as Christ and his Apostles did institute and practice in the Gospel.[38]

The destination of this increased desire for holiness and corporateness was congregational autonomy, at least in matters of faith. Beyond that it was Separatism. The Puritan approximation of the visible to the invisible Church was capable of being carried to a logical conclusion in voluntaryism; but voluntaryism derived less from individualism than from the idea of communal saintliness (i.e., congregationalism), and the yearning for a meaningful fellowship in worship.

The secularization that Anglican doctrine imposed on the Church cemented its Erastianism. That the Elizabethan Settlement marked the high water of ecclesiastical subservience to the State is a truism. With the notable exception of Grindal, whose fate was sequestration, the Anglican clergy were strictly obedient to royal authority. Their works abound in exhortations to obedience. A spiritualized Church, on the other hand, became a vantage for ecclesiastical assertiveness. James I's epigram "No Bishop, no King" was a gross distortion of Puritan hopes at the time; nevertheless it did represent a tendency, a tendency which culminated in that abortive and traumatic theocratic experiment of the Interregnum, the Parliament of Saints. Whereas Anglican

---

* To call Jacobs' *Principles* an Independent catechism is to follow the opinions of Champlin Burrage (*The Early English Dissenters in the Light of Recent Research*, 2 vols., Cambridge, 1912, Vol. I, Ch. 12) and George Yule (*The Independents in the English Civil War and Interregnum*, Cambridge, 1958, Ch. 1) that Jacobs, rather than Robert Browne, was the founder of Congregationalism.

doctrine encouraged the Church to become society-embraced, Puritan doctrine wanted the Church to be society-embracing.

These broad trends diverged specifically in habits of Church discipline. Both parties granted the State a coercive function in religion, for that, after all, was ancillary to their remaining church-type institutions. The problem was to determine the limits of the State's power; and on this point a range of answers existed, from Anglicans to Independents, that progressively increased the exclusion of State officers, or magistrates, from Church affairs. According to Whitgift, "the civil magistrate may not take upon him such ecclesiastical functions as are only proper to the minister of the church, as preaching of the Word, administering the sacraments, excommunicating, and such like; but that he hath no authority to make and execute laws for the church in things pertaining to the church, as discipline, ceremonies, etc. (so that he do nothing against the Word of God), though the papists affirm it never so stoutly, yet is the contrary most true, and sufficiently proved by men of notable learning, as Master Jewel, bishop of Salisbury, Master Horne, bishop of Winchester, Master Nowel, dean of St. Paul's."[39]

Against this, Cartwright stripped the magistrates of all initiatory power. "The prince and civil magistrates hath to see that the laws of God, touching his worship, and touching all matters and orders of the church be executed and duly observed, and to see that every ecclesiastical person do that office whereunto he is appointed, and to punish those which fail in their office accordingly. As for the making of orders and ceremonies of the church, they do (where there is a constituted and ordered church) pertain to the ministers of the church, and to the ecclesiastical governors; and that, and they meddle not in the making of civil laws, and laws for the commonwealth, so the civil magistrate hath not to ordain ceremonies pertaining to the church; but if those to whom that doth appertain make any orders not meet, the magistrate may and ought to hinder them, and drive them to better, forasmuch as the civil magistrate hath the charge to see that nothing be done against the glory of God in his dominion."[40]

In practice, the Puritans in the House of Commons went far beyond the mere recommendation of reform in Church matters, but Cartwright's statement suggests the principle. Civil government had a suspensive and advisory role only. Apart from that, its function was executive: the magistrates were the enforcing agents, and the "ministers, seniors, and deacons" alone had the right to initiate policy.

The Independents' attitude was similar to the Presbyterians', though with a slightly different emphasis. In the interests of civil law and order, they admitted the magistrates' coercive power over outward actions, but at the same time stressed liberty of conscience, or inward liberty. As Henry Ireton put it, "[the magistrate] hath not power to conclude your inward, but your outward man."[41] The Independents promised a sparing use of ecclesiastical discipline, but where it was used, like the Presbyterians, they granted an executive role to the State. Since, as the Leveller Overton pointed out, inward liberty was easily overridden by civil strength, the last was the operative concession.[42]

A significant rift, then, occurred between the Anglicans and the Puritans, the former yielding ecclesiastical initiative to the State, the latter reserving religious settlement (as a special case of the interpretation of God's Word) to Church authorities.

Why this difference? Whitgift's explanation was that the Puritans made a false distinction between the Church and the State, whereas he perceived "no such distinction of the commonwealth and the church that they should be counted, as it were, two several bodies, governed with divers laws and divers magistrates, except the church be linked with an heathenish and idolatrous commonwealth."[43] For his part, Cartwright accused Whitgift of what he willingly admitted: "I say, first, that he [Whitgift] stumbleth at one stone, which is, that he cannot put a difference between the church and the commonwealth, and so between church-officers . . . and the officers of the commonwealth, those which are ecclesiastical, and those which are civil."[44]

In short, Anglicanism did not distinguish between Church and State, whereas Puritanism did. A one-kingdom theory collided with a two-kingdom view. Hence the opposite tendencies:

in Anglicanism, to exploit the Church as a civil department; in Puritanism, to use the State as a religious instrument. Hence, too, the different understandings of "discipline" as a mark of a true Church: for Anglicans it meant outward conformity, for Puritans the ferreting-out of sin. At a deeper level, these distinctions followed naturally from theologies that secularized or spiritualized the Church. And, ultimately, those constructions rested on concepts of grace in relation to nature: the Anglicans' vision of a complementary hierarchy contrasted with the Puritans' feeling of continuous tension between the spheres.

The two trends of disciplinary convention are illustrated by the Puritans' and the Anglicans' respective attitudes toward excommunication. The Puritans constantly attacked the Anglicans for debasing the ultimate sanction by too frequent usage. "In those days [of the primitive Church]," ran the First Admonition, "it was the last censure of the church, and never went forth but for notorious crimes. Now it is pronounced for every light trifle. Then, excommunication was greatly regarded and feared; now, because it is a money matter, no whit at all esteemed."[45] This refers to the stricture for non-payment of fees. Whitgift had approved a form of civil excommunication that could be pronounced by the magistrate; he also allowed the ecclesiastical courts jurisdiction over contracts (marriage, divorce, wills and testaments, and the like), with power to excommunicate for refusal to meet money penalties—all of which aroused Cartwright's anger, for he considered such matters to be strictly civil.[46] The Millenary Petition of 1604 asked "that none be excommunicated for trifles and for twelvepenny matters."[47] In 1640, the Root and Branch Petition deplored "the general abuse of that great ordinance of excommunication, which God hath left in His Church as the last and greatest punishment which the Church can inflict on obstinate and great offenders." "Prelates," it continued, "do daily excommunicate men . . . for vain, idle, and trivial matters, as working, or opening a shop on a holy day, for not appearing at every beck upon their summons, not paying a fee, or the like . . . so that sacred ordinance of God . . . becomes contemptible."[48] There was more here than special pleading. The Puritans protested because they felt the Anglicans were debasing a religious weapon, were secularizing it and using it to impose conformity. Puritans wished to reserve ex-communication for "fit" offenders, and by this means to reinvest it with real spiritual meaning.

Calvinist Church polity was consistent with the doctrine of the Church suffused by grace. As we have seen, this belief contributed to congregational involvement by stressing the idea of the communion of saints. The polity of Presbyterianism is generally well understood: congregations selected ministers (or could veto the patron's choice) and elected elders who shared in the administration of the Church at all levels as coequals with the ministers. The quality of participation was the outstanding characteristic of the Calvinist form. This fact seems obvious enough, yet to assert it involves some qualification of current views.

It is frequently suggested that Calvinist polity answered the economic aspirations of the bourgeoisie (whoever they were). One would have little quarrel with this theory if it did not then proceed to specify the particular coincidences of form with class interests, and to hint that these caused the conversion of a new category of person. First, it is said that Calvinism offered the middle classes an opportunity to exert spiritual and moral influence over the Church membership, since they commanded the positions of eldership. Second, it is claimed that the doctrine of predestination was easily turned into a justification for worldly success: the Biblical promise that all things would be added to those who, first, had sought the Kingdom of God was perverted to uphold affluence as *prima facie* evidence of godliness.

This second assertion is a small facet of Weber's well-known theory of the Protestant ethic, as modified by Professor Tawney.[49] Negatively it may be important that Protestantism never made a virtue of poverty, but, as we noted in Chapter 1, it is dangerous to apply the doctrine of predestination too widely. The bourgeoisie have found respectable justification in any system—the capitalists of fifteenth-century Italy in Roman Catholicism, the industrialists of nineteenth-century Germany in Lutheranism.

The situation in the sixteenth century was no different: members of the English middle classes turned either to Anglicanism or to Puritanism, the merchants and financiers of Antwerp remained Catholics, and the relatively stagnant Scots adopted Presbyterianism. In other words, the second connection is an incidental relationship, not a necessary one.

The first connection has more truth in it: classes were potentially powerful engines of discipline. But it is hard to imagine that Puritans objected to Anglicanism because it did not permit the bourgeoisie to exert enough influence. For one thing, I would hesitate to link the middle class with Puritanism until after the Restoration, when the workings of the Clarendon Code (1661–65) crystallized a correlation. By then, too, the power latent in Presbyterianism had dissipated; for it could have become effective only if the system had been a national one. It is fascinating to explore the interaction of ideological structures with political or economic pressures, but it is a pastime to be indulged in with care.

Still, a problem remains: the correlation of the petty bourgeoisie with Separatism demands an explanation. Strictly speaking, Separatism is outside our realm of inquiry, but insofar as it took over, and even increased, the Calvinist emphasis on participation, it merits comment. This class-church phenomenon is still with us, though in the seventeenth century the petty bourgeoisie were tinkers, tailors, soldiers, sailors, butchers, bakers, and candlestick makers. Independency moved toward Separatism because it emphasized the communal aspect of Puritanism. The Sects carried those doctrines further; their Separatism was the result of an even greater desire for enthusiastic fellowship. Since this heightened degree of participation contrasts with the Sectaries' social circumstances, it seems plausible to think that their religious organization compensated them for social and political rejection.

In the extreme Sects, participation in the Church became the total substitute for unsatisfying civil experience: religion was life. In other cases, civil activity and religion complemented each other. It was the urge to participate that spurred on the Levellers' political organization, while Sectarian worship provided a religious outlet for the same urge. John Lilburne, for instance, found solace for political failure in Quakerism. So not only may we cull Leveller policies from Separatist worship; we can also trace both to the social needs of the petty bourgeoisie. By social needs, something larger than immediate economic interests is understood; perhaps human needs would be an apter phrase. Demonstrably, Leveller arguments contain the clamors of a class; but Sectarian worship served a broader and deeper need —namely, that of belonging to a group, man's gregarious and self-assertive instincts. Thus A. S. P. Woodhouse's brilliant exercise suggesting that Levellers applied an analogy between the segregated spheres of the Church and the State needs to be supplemented by a principle of sociological compensation: participation in the Church filled the gap of social as well as political non-enfranchisement.*

It has also been said that Puritan institutions were egalitarian, democratic, and individualistic.[50] This statement illuminates Puritanism in relation to Anglicanism, but it is not wholly applicable, for there was a hierarchical quality in Calvinism. Being comprehensive, the visible Church contained its quota of hypocrites; and the elect, though equally elected, might stand at various levels of faith. A saved man was ruled by two contrary forces, grace and nature—that cosmic struggle was waged in each chosen soul. As Perkins said, "When faith prevaileth, unbelief decayeth: neither can faith ever be perfect, because it is ever mingled more or less with unbelief."[51] Richard Sibbes, in *A Fountain Sealed* (1637), explained that "there are divers degrees of the Spirit sealing." He goes on: "The spirit sealeth by degrees; as our care of pleasing the Spirit increaseth, so our comfort increaseth, our light will increase as the morning light."[52] Despite initial equality, there could be an inequality of development in grace: some grew more gracious than others.

---

* This hypothesis may be fruitfully applied to Scotland, where, according to our principle of compensation, Puritanism was particularly vigorous because of the dourness of Scottish social and economic life. Some groundwork has been done by Sidney A. Burrell, "Calvinism, Capitalism, and the Middle Classes," *Journal of Modern History*, XXXII (1960), 129–31.

This assumption of unequal degrees of grace was reflected in the selection of deacons, elders, and ministers. Cartwright drew the contemporary analogy we would normally expect from an Anglican: "For the church is governed with that kind of government which the philosophers that write of the best commonwealth affirm to be the best. For in respect of the head, it is a monarchy; and in respect of the ancients [elders] and pastors that govern in common and with authority among themselves it is an aristocracy, or the rule of the best men; and in respect that the people are not secluded, but have their interests in church matters, it is a democracy or popular estate. An image whereof appeareth also in the policy of this realm."[53] It would be ignoring the evidence to deny a carry-over from Church to State in Puritan thinking; but the effect of the transfer should not be thought of as "democratic" without serious reservation. In a letter to Lord Say and Seal in 1636, John Cotton outlined his view of a State properly modeled on the Church: "Mr. Hooker doth often quote a saying of Mr. Cartwright . . . that no man fashioneth his house to his hangings, but his hangings to the house. It is better that the commonwealth be fashioned to the setting forth of God's house, which is the church: than to accommodate the Church frame to the civil state. Democracy I do not conceive that ever God did ordain as a fit government either for church or commonwealth. If the people be governors, who shall be governed? As for monarchy, and aristocracy, they are both of them clearly approved, and directed in Scripture."[54] The evidence indicates that echelons of holiness were presupposed by Puritanism, and that instead of equalitarianism we should stress the willing coadjuvancy, the vital quality of participation, in the Puritans' idea of Church structure.

Similarly, the Puritan doctrine of Christian liberty was not altogether the democratic force it has been assumed to be. It proclaimed the freedom of the chosen individual from the burdens of the law, yet originally it had but faint color of *laissez-faire* in it. To think of the doctrine as "freedom from interference" infuses it with an anachronism. Freedom from State control was a plea necessitated by the circumstances of Established conformity to realize the primary goal: in this sense, one had to cry freedom against intransigent opposition to obtain true Christian liberty. This may sound paradoxical, and, indeed, paradox was the heart of the matter. Christian liberty meant those privileges gained through obedience to the Gospel and to God's will. With obedience came the dispensations of grace that removed those who believed from the duress of punishment and death. St. Paul developed this paradox in his Epistle to the Galatians, and it appears in Ephesians: only voluntary obedience to the Gospel's concept of love and to the will of God could free men from the tutelage of the law; only this obedience could enable men to initiate truly righteous acts. It is freedom for, rather than freedom from.

The pressure toward conformity in Presbyterianism—as stringent from within as Anglicanism was from above—can be better understood in the light of Paul's injunctions. And the Pauline paradox is the most satisfying explanation for Cromwell's curious notion of liberty, expressed in the speech to his first Protectorate Parliament (1654). "I said: you were a Free Parliament, and truly so you are—whilst you own the Government and Authority which called you hither."[55] Parliament, he was saying, could rise above its carnal fetters once it acknowledged the witness of providences that certified him, the Protector, as God's chosen instrument. Parliament should obey him as such. Clearly, Christian liberty did not intend individualism, or anything like it; rather, it bolstered authoritarianism. While the emphasis was less on "freedom" than on "power through obedience," the doctrine was a potential justification for tyranny. But since rival minorities struggling for power must cry liberty in the unshackling sense, the doctrine became so entangled with political necessity, and so extended, that it could develop from its religious obedience meaning to the idea of *laissez-faire* in the Civil War and Interregnum. Thus the Sectaries used it at one moment to claim toleration in the sphere of nature, and at another to brace their intolerance in the sphere of grace—inviting voluntary obedience to the Gospel ethic as they understood it. According to this view, which runs contrary to the trend of modern interpretation, "liberty" arrived as much in spite of, as because of, the Puritans' doctrine of Christian liberty.

Finally, individualism should be viewed in the context of the hegemony that absorbed it; for individuality was consumed by the urge to identify with the congregation. In other words, Puritan individualism was that of the group—a highly cellular phenomenon.

Above all, participation was the keynote of Puritan organization. Puritans were subject to a process of conditioning in their religious life that had obvious implications for everyday economic and political affairs. Indeed, the long constitutional struggle could be interpreted as a corollary of Puritanism's doctrinally conditioned urge to participate in the Church.

Like the Puritans, the Anglicans thought that their polity resembled the structure of civil society, the difference being that Puritanism presumed degrees of grace while Anglicanism raised a tangible ladder of order. The sneers of Anglicans at the leveling, democratic way of Puritanism reveal a partial inability to understand their opposition: their indictments, though warranted by the visible evidence, failed to take into account the Puritan concept of the Church as a spiritual society. Anglicans could not sympathize with anything but a visible Church orientation. Appropriately, their arguments for episcopacy were relative and experimental. "I conclude," wrote Whitgift, "that in the Scriptures there is no certain form prescribed for electing ministers, and that the doings of the apostles in these matters are not at all times of necessity to be followed; but it is sufficient to respect their end and purpose, that is, that there be meet ministers; and therefore M. Beza saith: 'No men may here prescribe any certain rule; but if the conscience be good, it is an easy matter to determine what is most expedient for time, place, and other circumstances.' "[56]

Hooker couched the same relativism in a bed of reason. "The truth is, that all the controversy in this cause concerning the orders of the church is, what particulars the church may appoint. That which doth find out is the force of man's reason. That which doth guide and direct his reason is first the general law of nature."[57] Further on, he added that "the nature of every law must be judged by the end for which it was made, and the aptness of things therein prescribed unto the same end."[58] Ecclesiastical polity was not decreed by Scripture, and so could be altered by men according to their needs.[59] This, broadly, represents one continuing stream of Anglican thought: episcopacy was the form most suited to existing circumstances. Since the argument employs as its criterion the internal consistency of Church polity with civil practice, we may call it, by a philosophical analogy, the coherence theory of government.

Richard Bancroft, in his celebrated sermon at St. Paul's Cross in 1588–89, advanced a correspondence theory of government: episcopacy conformed to the absolute (*a priori*) dictates of Scripture.[60] From an Anglican this was a startling assertion, since it opposed the usual coherence theory; moreover, it was precisely the argument of the Puritans themselves. Now no longer could there be a dialectic between Puritans and Anglicans who held this ground, for their convictions led only to assertions and counterassertions.[61] It was, of course, singularly appropriate and hardly surprising that the chief prosecutor of Puritanism should discover such a clever rebuttal; however, given the prolonged controversy, it was surely an inevitable shift to turn Puritan artillery against Puritans—sooner or later someone would have done it.

Bancroft's inspiration failed to transform Anglican thinking. The coherence tradition continued—indeed, Bancroft himself used it in polemic cheek by jowl with his new theory[62]—but at least a fresh argument, and more heat, were introduced into the conflict. Even Hooker, who belonged to the other tradition, murmured that the Scriptures called for the rule of bishops, but he did not elaborate.[63] It was left to Jacobean divines—Field, Overall, Andrewes, Cosin, Montagu, Laud, and their like—to pursue the argument more vigorously.

Despite the efforts of Anglo-Catholics to think otherwise, the argument for episcopacy *jure divino,* ordained by God, rested on the Scriptures, the practice of the apostles, and the continuation of that form throughout history; it never depended on a strict doctrine of apostolic succession.[64] Post-Restoration high churchmanship must have developed with the exiles during the Interregnum, for one finds little trace of it before the Civil War.

Laud, for example, distinguished himself from both Romans and Puritans. "And a great trouble it is to them [Puritans] that we maintain that our calling of Bishop is *Jure Divino,* by Divine Right: Of this I have said enough . . . nor will I repeat. Only this I will say, and abide by it, that the Calling of Bishops is *Jure Divino,* by Divine Right, though not all the Adjuncts to their calling. And this I say in as direct opposition to the Church of Rome, as to the Puritan humour.

"And I say further, that from the Apostles' times, in all ages, in all places, the Church of Christ was governed by Bishops: And Lay-Elders never heard of till Calvin's new-fangled device at Geneva."[65] Scripture was the basis as much of the Anglican view as of the Calvinist. According to Andrewes, "this was the order while Christ was upon the earth, Christ himself; the twelve, whose successors were bishops; the seventy, whose successors were priests." But he came to this conclusion only after he had cited and synthesized an intricate list of Biblical passages.[66]

The discovery of episcopacy in Scripture seemed a natural outgrowth of the controversy, yet the ramifications of the issue could hardly have been predicted. A few began to see episcopacy as an inviolable form of a true Church. More generally, it was considered vastly superior to alternative systems, and necessary to the perfection of a Church if not part of its essence. In 1610, Scottish ministers required no special episcopal ordination before being consecrated as bishops. At this date, Anglicans regarded Presbyterianism in Scotland as a foreign Church that had been prevented from having bishops by adverse historical circumstances. At least, such was Bancroft's judgment. Later, Laud placed Scotland in the category of a domestic Church, with a matching stiffening of attitude. Not many people, though, were as extreme as Jeremy Taylor or Richard Montagu, the latter maintaining that "there is no priesthood except in the Church, and no Church without a priestly order"[67]—a principle that unchurched non-episcopal Reformed Churches. Once again, a watershed must be sought in the Interregnum: for after the Restoration, when Scottish divines were sent to England to become bishops, two who had not received episcopal ordination were required first to become deacons, then priests. By that time, Scotland was treated as a schematical section of the Established communion.[68]

The net result of the correspondence theory for Anglicanism was to spiritualize the framework of the Church, to canonize its structure, as it were, while the Church body itself remained visible. This strain of development inevitably led to an increasing intransigence toward the Presbyterian and Independent orders; it also nudged Anglicanism into closer empathy with Rome. For all their wild exaggerations, Puritans were right to fear a shift toward Rome in the defense of the hierarchy. After the Restoration, Richard Baxter noticed ruefully that whereas Presbyterian clergy who wished to become Anglicans had to be reordained, Roman Catholic priests were accepted at par.[69]

Belief in the divine institution of episcopacy proved the chief stumbling block to Presbyterian conformity at the Restoration, since Puritans resented it more than anything else. For Anglicans the principle was an *entrée* to Anglo-Catholicism; and it remains to this day an obstruction to unity between Protestant branches. At the Lambeth Conference of 1948, the Committee on Unity reported at length: "Unity in practice has not ruled out a certain diversity of interpretation. Some, holding episcopacy to be of the *esse* of the Church, are bound by their convictions to hold that non-episcopal ministries are not ministries of the Church, and lack that authoritative commission, without which there can be no guaranteed priestly ministrations. Others, while holding firmly that episcopacy is the normal method for the transmission of ministerial authority, yet feel themselves bound, in view of the manifest blessing of God on non-episcopal ministries, to recognize those ministries as true ministries and their sacraments as true sacraments. Yet others hold shades of opinion intermediate between these two views. It is clear that in any scheme for reunion or intercommunion all these views must be recognized and allowed for. To treat non-episcopal ministries as identical in status and authority with the episcopal ministry rules out the first of the two views mentioned above. To declare the sacraments of non-episcopal bodies to be null and void rules out the second. It follows . . . that the acceptance of episcopacy as part of the life of the Church, and of episcopal ordination as the rule of Church, is a prerequisite for the formation of a United Church with Anglican participation, or for the establishment of rules of inter-communion."[70]

The clerics of the seventeenth century laid precedents more lasting than they knew. Understandably, Puritans found episcopacy *jure divino* intolerably galling, and their anger case-hardened the certainties of their antagonists. In this way the conflict between the Puritans' spiritual view of the Church and the Anglicans' visible interpretation was intensified beyond reconciliation by the Divine Righters' sanctification of episcopal structure.

Chapter 3 Sacraments and Eschatology

Sacraments

"And whereas this meat is called by Paul spiritual, it is signified that sacraments are no common signs, as though none of these things which are signified were received: for then they should be but external and earthly meats, and not spiritual. Further, God mocks not, nor deceives, that he would promise anything in the sacraments which he will not perform by any means. Yet neither is there need of a metamorphosis (which they call transubstantiation) to the end that the sacrament should become spiritual food. We ought not to confound the nature of the signs with the things signified. Let us follow the mean and sound way; and let us judge honourably of the sacraments—not thinking them to be things altogether empty of spiritual good, nor so joining the signs with the things that they pass wholly into them. It is enough to appoint a profitable and most excellent signification, by which the faithful mind, through believing, may be made partaker of the things signified."[1]

Peter Martyr (1500–1562), from whom this quotation comes, has been chosen to represent the Reformed doctrine of the sacraments partly because he was an acknowledged authority on sacramental theology,[2] and partly because he was respected by Anglicans and Puritans alike. Indeed, on the explicit theology of the sacraments, we should not think of Anglicans and Puritans as distinct, for they held a number of views in common. First, both categorically rejected transubstantiation, or the physical change of the elements into the actual and material Body and Blood of Christ. Laud, whom some would call an Anglo-Catholic, denounced transubstantiation as a fundamental error: "For transubstantiation . . . that was never heard of in the primitive church, nor till the Council of Lateran, nor can it be proved out of Scripture; and, taken properly, cannot stand with the grounds of Christian religion."[3] The great Puritan casuist Perkins discarded it for similar reasons.[4] At points, Perkins' discussion seems a carbon copy of Martyr's: "Although in a sacrament there must be a distinction between the sign and the things signified, yet [Papists] make none, but overthrow all signification of the signs by their transubstantiation."[5] Laud would have agreed that the supposed metamorphosis was "a magical fiction."[6]

Second, both the Anglican and the Puritan arguments against transubstantiation jettisoned consubstantiation—the position adopted by Luther—which held Christ's corporal Body and Blood to be coexistent with the bread and wine. The Anglicans were reluctant to attack Luther because he had fathered the Reformation; nevertheless, they carefully distinguished his position both from the Romans' and from their own, and very gently repudiated it.[7] "The bread," wrote Cranmer, "is exalted to the name of the Lord's body, after the sanctification, and yet the nature of the bread remaineth still; which cannot be . . . if the body of Christ were then present."[8] Cranmer was no Lutheran even though Osiander was his father-in-law. The Puritans behaved toward Luther with equal tact. "All the controversy," cautioned Perkins, "lies in the manner of receiving; we contenting ourselves with that spiritual receiving which is by the hand of faith, they [Lutherans] adding thereto the corporal."[9]

Third, Anglicans and Puritans were equally intolerant of the doctrine that described the sacramental elements as mere signs or figures. Their position on this point proves the error of two common claims: one, that Cranmer was a Zwinglian;* and, two, that the sacraments in Puritanism were purely symbolic celebrations. Cranmer complained of misrepresentation in his own times, and his protest still needs to be heeded today. "Do I say in my book that those which come to the Lord's table do 'eat nothing else, but only bare bread of corn, and mere wine of the grape' —Who saith so, good sir?—How often do I teach and repeat again and again, that as corporally with our mouths we eat and

---

* Zwinglianism preached a memorial doctrine of sacraments. Sacraments were only signs of grace; they did not confer it. "A sacrament is a sign of a sacred thing—i.e., of grace that has been given. I believe that it is a visible figure or form of invisible grace." "Sacraments are so far from conferring grace that they do not even convey or distribute it." *Reckoning of the Faith of Huldreich Zwingli to the Roman Emperor Charles,* in S. M. Jackson, *Huldreich Zwingli* (New York, 1901), Appendix.

drink the sacramental bread and wine, so spiritually with our hearts, by faith, do we eat Christ's very flesh, and drink his very blood, and do both feed and live spiritually by him, although corporally he be absent from us . . . as in baptism we come not unto the water as we come unto other common waters, when we wash our hands, or bathe our bodies, but we know that it is a mystical water."[10] Cranmer's protest needs no comment; presumably those who would saddle him with Zwinglianism have not read him.[11]

Calvin was no less opposed to Zwinglianism. "The Lord bids us take bread and wine. At the same time he declares that he gives the spiritual nourishment of his flesh and blood."[12] He continues: "It is declared in my writings more than a hundred times, that so far am I from rejecting the term substance [of Christ], that I ingenuously and readily declare, that by the incomprehensible agency of the Spirit, spiritual life is infused into us from the substance of the flesh of Christ. I also constantly admit that we are all substantially fed on the flesh and blood of Christ though I discard the gross fiction of a local intermingling."[13] The essence of Calvin's and, more immediately, of Knox's doctrine is written in the Scots Confession of 1560, which lays down that the elements are never to be regarded as "bot naked and baire signes."[14] Against such evidence the error that ascribes a simple memorialist view to Puritanism cannot stand.

Fourth, in another sense, both Anglicans and Puritans did regard the sacraments as symbols. The memorial aspect of the sacrament ("This do in remembrance of me"), as distinct from a doctrine holding it to be a mere memorial act, was recognized in the prayer of consecration in *The Book of Common Prayer*. In the Directory of Public Worship (1645) the emphasis occurred at the breaking of bread. The Savoy Declaration of Faith and Order (1658) stressed the commemorative nature of sacrament, to oust the idea of real sacrifice, in its chapter on the Lord's Supper.[15] Even Arminians like Andrewes were clear about the sacrament's symbolic significance: "Of the sacraments we may say *Hoc erit signum*. For a sign it is . . . and a sign . . . for Christ in the sacrament is not altogether unlike Christ in the cratch [manger]. To the cratch we may well like the husk or outward symbols of it. Outwardly it seems little worth but it is rich of content, as was the crib . . . with Christ in it. For what are they . . . 'weak and poor elements' of themselves? Yet in them we find Christ."[16] Andrewes' touching metaphor clarifies metaphysical theology: elements were at once figures and infinitely more than figures. This truth was underlined by that rigid Independent John Owen in his *Discourses on the Lord's Supper*: "Neither is there in this ordinance a naked figure, a naked representation: there is something in the figure, something in the representation, but there is not all in it."[17]

For, fifth, according to both groups, the figures of bread, wine, and baptismal water were accompanied—divines were not specific about how and where—by an energizing grace that transformed them truly into flesh, blood, and divine transfusion for believing spirits. John Cosin, the Arminian, maintained "that the Body and Blood of Christ are sacramentally and really (not feignedly) present when the Bread and Wine are taken by the faithful communicants."[18] Owen believed Christ was exhibited as "flesh and meat indeed," and tendered Himself as a man tenders payment to be received into the coffers of the soul "for these two ends: for incorporation, for nourishment."[19] Latimer's explanation to the judges at his trial was representative: "I say there is none other presence of Christ required than a spiritual presence . . . and the same presence may be called a real presence, because to the faithful there is the real or spiritual body of Christ."[20]

Finally, both Puritans and Anglicans regarded the sacraments as an efficacious means of grace, or (to use Andrewes' image) vehicles of the Spirit, "the proper carriages" to grace.[21] Hooker, believing "that grace is a consequence of sacraments, a thing which accompanieth them as their end," anticipated the Presbyterian Baxter, who thought sacraments were appointed "to be [Christ's] agents, without, and his Spirit within, effectually to communicate his grace."[22] In short, sacraments were at one and the same time commemorations and participations in grace with a living Christ by virtue of His real spiritual presence in the consecrated elements.

So far, contemporaries have been allowed to speak for themselves. The quotations have been drawn from prominent Puritans, and from both moderate and Arminian Anglicans, to demonstrate that the theological mean between the Zwinglian and Lutheran views of sacrament was the common doctrine of both parties. If this conclusion is correct, the antagonism between Puritan and Anglican cannot be explained in terms of sacramental theology as such. C. W. Dugmore's useful compendium of English eucharistic doctrine is positively misleading when it distinguishes Puritan opinion from Anglican by describing the former as "Receptionist," or neo-Zwinglian.[23] The distinction is unreal.

Yet one may see, impressionistically, an inclination in Puritanism toward a more simplistic commemorative view of the sacrament, and in Anglicanism a tendency to emphasize the qualities of spiritual involvement and sacrifice. Laud's talk of sacrifice, however, had nothing to do with propitiatory sacrifice: it was merely an "offering up" of commemoration, of praise and thanksgiving, and of rededication—an interpretation, he rightly affirmed, acceptable to the Puritans.[24] The Puritan attitude was stated by William Perkins. As was his manner, Perkins propounded, then expounded: sacrifice was "a sacred or solemn action; in which man offereth and consecrateth some outward bodily thing unto God for this end, to please and humour him." "The supper of the Lord is a sacrifice, and may truly be called so as it hath been in former ages; and that in three respects. 1. Because it is a memorial of the real sacrifice of Christ upon the cross, and contains withal a thanksgiving to God for the same. . . . 2. Because every communicant doth there present himself body and soul, a living, holy and acceptable sacrifice unto God. . . . 3. It is called a sacrifice in respect of that which was joined with the sacrament, namely, the alms given to the poor as a testimony of our thankfulness unto God."[25]

Between Laud and Perkins there was no essential difference; and yet there was a slight difference of emphasis, as if the Puritans said to the Anglicans, "We accept your notion of sacrifice, but prefer not to bandy the term about because it is fraught with superstition." This was a scarcely perceptible shift of viewpoint, rather than a rift of principle. But let us hasten to add that, overtly, any distance between the two parties was minimal before the Civil War.

Covertly, however, Anglicans and Puritans were decisively separated in their views. The chief difference concerned the practical efficacy of the sacraments, incompatible estimates being made of their effects. This pragmatic aspect of sacramental doctrine has received scant attention; yet it makes a revealing study, for the conceptions of the benefits accruing from the sacraments acted as undertows to explicit theology.

For Anglicans, sacraments were a conspicuously effective means of grace, whereas Puritans (true to their view of man) stressed prevenient grace, and so mitigated the impact of the grace that came by way of the sacraments. One cardinal test was baptism—an issue thoroughly canvassed by the Admonitors Field and Wilcox, together with Cartwright, against Whitgift and Hooker. Surprisingly, or perhaps not surprisingly given the prevailing secularism of historians, the problem has received virtually no attention. I propose to use the controversy as an archetype for the whole period, a justifiable device insofar as it occupied the central years of ecclesiastical disharmony and contained both the past and the future. The arguments hinged upon two questions: the fate of the infant dying unbaptized; and the administration of private baptism. The second was complicated by the fact that private baptism was usually celebrated by a midwife, which raised the propriety of women administering sacramental rites.*

With regard to the fate of the child dying unbaptized, we have the rare spectacle of a Puritan accusing St. Augustine of absurdity.[26] Cartwright was unequivocal: infants without the sacrament were not condemned because they lacked it, and he

---

* Cartwright believed that the ministry of Word and Sacrament had been inseparably joined by God, and that preaching had to accompany sacraments to make them effective; both of these conditions precluded women from baptizing, and both of them were flatly denied by Whitgift. Clearly, this issue about women affected attitudes toward baptism in general; but to avoid complicating the discussion further, I have omitted the question from the text, leaving it to be reflected in the various references in the Notes.

quoted Calvin in explanation.[27] "The truth is . . . that if he be
not a Christian before he came to receive baptism, baptism can
make him no Christian, which is only the seal of the grace of
God before received."[28] The grace of God "before received,"
given prior to sacrament, is, of course, what is called prevenient
grace. It is a formula demanded by Puritanism's stress on man's
total depravity: it underlined justification by faith (a person
could not perform anything to save himself), and also the sovereignty of God, who forechose His elect. The practical and
logical upshot of reliance on prevenient grace was to derogate
the efficacy of sacrament.[29] This, at least, was Whitgift's allega-
tion, and whatever allowance we make for Whitgift's desire to
score debating points, the substance of his charge remains true;
moreover, it reveals his own predilection to lay more faith on
sacrament. "Your manner of doctrine is such that it maketh men
think that the external signs of the sacraments are base ceremonies and in no sense necessary to salvation; which must in
time bring in a contempt of the sacrament, and especially of
baptism for infants."[30]

Anglicanism entertained grave doubts about the fate of
the unbaptized. According to Whitgift, they would probably,
though not inevitably, be damned: "What Christian would willingly suffer his child to die without the sacrament of regeneration, the lack whereof (though it be not necessary) yet may it
seem to be a probable token and sign of reprobation."[31] Hooker
skillfully discarded the concept of prevenient grace in order to
attribute saving effects entirely to the sacrament: "Let us never
think it safe to presume of our own last end, by bare conjectural
collections of His first intent and purpose, the means failing
that should come between. Predestination bringeth not to life,
without the grace of external vocation, wherein our baptism is
implied. For as we are not naturally men without birth, so
neither are we Christian men in the eye of the Church of God
but by new birth, nor according to the manifest ordinary course
of divine dispensation new-born, but by that baptism which
both declareth and maketh us Christians. In which respect we
justly hold it to be the door of our actual entrance into God's
house, the first apparent beginning of life, a seal perhaps to the

grace of Election, before received, but to our own sanctification
here a step that hath not any before it."[32] In exact contrast to the
Puritans, the Anglicans enhanced the effect of sacrament by
disregarding prevenient grace.

Answers to the second question, whether private baptism be
admitted or no, yield consistent findings. The two Admonitions
denounced private baptisms out of hand, leaving Cartwright to
supply the reasons.[33] Cartwright made three points: first and
most important, the sacraments were essentially congregational
activities (we meet Puritanism's congregational ethos again and
again); second, there was never a necessity for emergency baptism; and, third, belief in its necessity implied the Roman superstition that salvation was tied to sacraments.[34]

The Anglican counter to the last point was really a veiled
capitulation: baptism did not cause regeneration; God did, but
it was the means and instrument of grace—a *sine qua non*. In
Hooker's words, "Although . . . we make not baptism a cause
of grace, yet the grace which is given them with their baptism
doth so far forth depend on the very outward sacrament, that
God will have it embraced not only as a sign or token what we
receive but also as an instrument or mean whereby we receive
grace."[35] The implication within this assessment is momentous:
nothing less than belief in a sacramental approach to grace.

Consequently, in the Anglican view, private baptism was a
necessity whenever imminent death prevented the arrangement
of a public service. Lack of baptism, in all likelihood, meant
damnation. To this was added the argument that God had in-
stituted baptism in Scripture, and surely His commands were
mandatory.[36] Incidentally, the Anglicans' recourse to Scripture
reinforces our suggestion that their total characterization as
traditionalists is outworn, though it still stands that their exe-
geses tended to be more patristic than the Puritans'.

Finally, when Cartwright argued that if baptism and communion could be private, why not preaching and other functions as well, Whitgift blandly answered, "Why not indeed—so
long as the law and order of the Church be duly observed!"[37]
Puritan congregationalism was flatly negated by the particularism we have already noted.

Despite Anglican taunts, Puritans were not prepared to follow the Baptists in dispensing with infant baptism altogether. However, the small importance they attached to the sacrament suggested Baptist leanings. In comparison, the Anglican expectation of baptism was immeasurably greater.

The same may be said about Anglican hopes of the Supper. Anglicanism regarded the Eucharist as a continuous means of faith—as if grace compounded with celebration. Jewel believed that "Christ's institution, and the mystical benediction which he called the quickening grace, continueth still. . . . For all sacraments have their virtue and power, not of themselves, but wholly and only from Christ. Wherefore, as Christ is one, and continueth still without change; even so must the grace that worketh in us by his sacraments be likewise one, and continue still."[38] If Jewel typified Elizabethan Anglicanism, Andrewes represented Jacobean Arminianism. He heightened Jewel's expectation by drawing out its implicit presumptions, likening the Eucharist to a spiritual recapitulation of the Gospel in the present. "For as there is a recapitulation of all in Christ in the holy sacrament . . . a kind of hypostatical union of the sign and the thing signified."[39] Andrewes' extreme reverence for communion is no new departure: it runs straight from the preconceptions of his predecessors, who assumed a sacramental way to grace. Their belief in the sacramental approach to Heaven included the intense veneration for the Eucharist that the Arminians displayed. And the quickening of the current in that direction may be laid to the intrinsically dialectical pressures of the ideological controversy in which Anglicans and Puritans were engaged.

Puritanism's assessment of the efficacy of the Eucharist was more modest. This does not mean that Puritans had a low view of the sacrament, for our argument has been that the doctrines were alike, but it does say that they held a lesser expectation of grace in the Supper. According to Calvin, the Eucharist merely authenticated the prevenient grace already given: "Sacraments are as it were, seals to seal the grace of God in our hearts and render it more authentic."[40] He desired frequent communion for its "ratifying" activity; justification was not the result of celebration, for God justified His chosen independently by confronting them with the Gospel (illuminated by the Holy Spirit), and once this grace was gained, the assurance of it was stead-fast.[41] The Eucharist could add little to this independent assurance; so it served as a stimulant and a corrective to faith.

A century later, Baxter had the same outlook. If he had been asked to state his doctrine, he could have passed unchallenged as an Anglican; but his underlying attitude was altogether different. It is revealed in his *Reformed Liturgy,* in which the order for celebrating the Supper was prefaced by lengthy injunctions for self-examination and acknowledgment of sin, an emphasis that outweighed the sense of grace inhering in the sacrament itself.[42] Similarly, the Directory for Public Worship made the Lord's Supper an opportunity for spiritual discipline rather than a feast of Holy participation.[43] Of course, this could not be otherwise, given a doctrine hung between the polarities of man's utter perversity and God's omnipotence.

By and large, the stated doctrines of Puritans and Anglicans were identical, yet their attitudes to the sacraments were radically dissimilar because their expectations of grace were remote from each other. Anglicans had a dynamic concept of sacramental power, and Puritans a static one.

These doctrinal undercurrents led to an inequality of focus on the sacraments in the church service: for Anglicans, they formed the heart of worship; for Puritans, they were peripheral. The Liturgy of 1559 and Advertisements of 1566, and later the Canons of 1604, establish how large a place sacraments were given by Convocation: the provisions for baptism were elaborate, and communion was to be celebrated frequently. Puritanism made no such stipulations. It is true that Calvin and Cartwright were in favor of frequent communion, but not for the same reasons that Anglicans advocated it. Calvin had desired weekly communion, since he saw it as an opportunity for imposing discipline; Anglicanism provided for more than weekly participations on demand,* since it regarded the sacrament as too valuable to be denied to any who requested it. In Scotland, Calvin's hopes were so far lost sight of that by the eighteenth century

---

* Feast days as well as Holy Days.

many parishes, by deliberate decision, did not celebrate the Eucharist more than once a year.[44]

The importance that Anglicans attached to these two sacraments is demonstrated, in the case of baptism, by the emphasis on urgency, and, in the case of communion, by the willingness to dispense it indiscriminately.[45] This prevailing non-selectivity was protested by the First Admonition: formerly, "they shut men by reason of their sins from the Lord's Supper. We thrust them in sin to the Lord's Supper."[46] Whitgift's retort mirrored his own high expectancy of sacrament: surely, he argued, we should compel men to communicate because of the spiritual benefits that might accrue to them;[47] after all, Judas had partaken with the twelve, though he had been a reprobate.[48] Puritanism's concern to weed out the unworthy reflects its low view of human nature, and its de-emphasis of communion, which was subsidiary to the original and independent covenant between God and man.*

Closely related to the doctrinal view of sacrament was the subjective appreciation of it by the participant. Of course it is impossible to establish a subjective state with subjective evidence (in history, if not in psychiatry), but the conclusion develops logically from the argument above. In Anglicanism, sacrament excited the individual *qua* sacrament, and in Puritanism, *qua* communion. We have already seen evidence of this in the quarrel over the words of distribution in the communion order (p. 42 above). Anglicans, we noted, defended a particular and individual directive, whereas Puritans demanded an inclusive congregational phrasing. Similarly, the quarrel over private baptism reflects the same difference, Cartwright claiming that sacraments had to be communal to be sacraments, and Whitgift replying that it was not necessarily so, that privacy was proper. More dramatically, the Arminians' adoration of God with the Eucharist suggests that sacrament thrilled them as sacrament. We know that Puritanism abominated their behavior, but that does not say the Eucharist was regarded with apathy by the individual

---

* Puritanism's desire for a restricted communion was, of course, linked with its conception of the Church as composed of converted persons.

Puritan. In Scotland, intense emotion surrounded the Lord's Supper, and on occasion it became an extra-congregational celebration, with neighboring parishes joining in.[49] However, it was the gathering and the fellowship, more than the sacrament *per se,* that fed Puritans' enthusiasm. This "communal" aspect of the Puritan celebration, limiting the "sacramental" aspect, made inevitably for the drift of emphasis to the memorial element contained in the larger doctrine.

Another major derivative of the divergent notions of sacramental power was a varying emphasis on preaching in the service. Anglicanism's dynamic view kept preaching from the core of worship. Its place in the Anglican scale of values is illustrated by Laud's speech at the Censure of John Bastwick, Henry Burton, and William Prynne (1637): "And you, my honourable Lords of the Garter, in your great solemnities, you do your reverence, and to Almighty God, I doubt it not; but yet it is *versus altare,* 'towards His altar,' as the greatest place of God's residence upon earth. (I say the greatest, yea, greater than the pulpit; for there 'tis *Hoc est corpus meum,* 'This is my body'; but in the pulpit 'tis at most but *Hoc est verbum meum,* 'This is My Word.' And a greater reverence, no doubt, is due to the body than to the word of our Lord.)"[50] Certainly Laud's veneration for the sacrament was extreme, but the Elizabethan Anglicans fought the issue to the same conclusion.

Puritanism, on the other hand, claimed that sacraments depended upon preaching, that without preaching there could be no valid sacrament (though an exposition need not precede celebration immediately). The Puritans' scale reversed the Anglican placement of sacrament above preaching; for them the independent covenant was critical. According to Whitgift, this arrangement devastated the centrality and efficacy of the sacraments.[51] Cartwright had declared: "This I say, that, when as the life of the sacraments dependeth of the preaching of the Word of God, there must of necessity the Word of God be, not read, but preached unto the people, amongst whom the sacraments are ministered." To which Whitgift replied: "If this doctrine of yours be true, then be the sacraments dead sacraments and with-

out effect, except the word be preached when they are ministered."[52] Jacobean Arminians weighted the scale heavily in favor
of the sacrament, but the balance had been tipped in that direction all the time. Anglicanism had always assumed the primacy
of the sacramental process, and Puritanism the transcending
importance of Gospel confrontation.

The ministerial orientations of Anglican and Puritan clergy
corresponded to their scales of value. Preaching necessarily took
its toll on the administrative and contemplative functions of
Puritan ministers; conversely, Anglican priests, less bothered
with preaching, were freer for those concerns. There were, of
course, exceptions to this rule—Andrewes and Donne were great
preachers—but it may stand in general. Preaching, by mouth or
by pen, was life for the Puritan; by the very precepts of his existence, he had to be a vehicle for the Word, a scale of values that
explains what Haller called Puritanism's "vital rage for utter-
ance."[53]

In contrast, we may gather from Andrewes' devotional *Praeces
Privatae,* Laud's immense administrative activity, or Donne's
introversion that preaching was not such a compulsion for Anglicans. We receive the same impression from the widespread
Anglican preference for reading Scripture rather than expound-
ing it. According to one view, this preference was simply a comfortable rationalization for the clerical ignorance that sprang
from the Church's economic poverty.[54] This may be part of the
explanation, but it is still possible that the unconcern with
preaching was connected with a security and self-satisfaction
engendered by a belief in the potency of the sacraments. If the
suggestion makes doctrine the devil, that is what is intended: to
relate these particular variations to profound differences in
soteriology.

Cartwright considered the mere reading of Scriptures a perversion of proper perspective: "And, although reading do help
to nourish the faith which cometh by preaching, yet [nourish-
ment] is given to preaching κατ' ἐξοχήν [par excellence] . . .
and for that it is the excellentest and most ordinary means to
work by in the hearts of hearers. The beholding of the creatures,

and the consideration of the making of the world, and of God's wisdom and wonderful love appearing in them, doth nourish and strengthen faith, and yet it may not therefore in efficacy be compared to the preaching of the word of God."[55] Preaching was not an isolated characteristic of Puritanism, but part and parcel of its deepest preconceptions; as such it dominated the attention of Puritans in the sixteenth and seventeenth centuries, and even now traces of the preference remain.

Insofar as Anglicanism regarded the Eucharist as a continuum of grace, it avoided Scriptural absolutism. Laud's statement quoted above is apropos: God's word was secondary to His sacrament. Indirectly, by providing a focus other than Scripture, this order of importance left the way open for assimilative rationality to be used in "matters indifferent" to salvation—a concession that may help to explain the continuance of that rational stream in Anglicanism which Puritanism submerged under Scriptural fundamentalism. It was not that Anglicanism was unscriptural, merely less rigidly so because more sacramental.

Another effect of the dynamic view of sacrament was to permit the rise of sacerdotalism. The clergy were neither mediators nor workers of miracles at the Eucharist, but because the sacraments they dispensed were imperative for salvation, their administrative status was commensurately enhanced. I do not mean to depict the whole Establishment as sacerdotal, but merely to suggest, tentatively, that underlying doctrine offered no hindrance to, and perhaps even encouraged, the emergence of the sacerdotal strain. The Laudians exemplify it. The stronger the sense of sacramental power, the greater the likelihood that priestly functions would become elevated. From another angle, the seeds of sacerdotalism lay dormant in the Anglicans' great expectations of the sacraments.

Finally, ritualism, and the development of ritualism, was the natural corollary to the dynamic view. If one believed that the Eucharist was the crowning act of worship, one would readily come to surround it with ritual: to receive kneeling rather than sitting; to bedeck the table with candles, crucifixes, and cloths; to keep the altar in the east end at a remove from the irreverent crowd; and to bow to the altar on entering church. These were the greatest but not the only grievances of Puritanism. Henry Burton's *Apology of an Appeal* (1636) and Prynne's multifarious attacks—from the brief *News from Ipswich* (1626) against Wren to his vast compilation of evidence against Laud in *Canterbury's Doom* (1646)—enumerate a catalogue of novel abuses, some of them negligible in themselves, but straws in the wind to the weatherwise. The immediate cause of Burton's and Prynne's complaints was the new *Book of Fasts,* issued at the time of the plague by a proclamation of October 18, 1636.[56]

The proclamation banned meetings in London and the suburbs for the duration of the plague, and reprinted the *Book of Fasts,* a book of prayers and instructions that was first issued in 1603. Prayers for seasonable weather and the Navy were omitted; a collect applauding preaching and England's deliverance from Romish superstition was passed over; Lady Elizabeth and her children were not mentioned in prayer; the word "in" was changed to "at" in the phrase "in the name of Jesus every knee shall bow"—a change designed to encourage curtseying; the second service was enjoined to be read from the communion table instead of from the pulpit; a specification of the Prince and his children as the Elect of God was forgotten; and the solemn warning against attributing merit to fasting was overlooked.

The substance of the proclamation, however, was the prohibition of gatherings in London and the suburbs, which, with the appointment of weekly fasts for Wednesdays, in fact amounted to a roundabout attempt to gag Puritan lecturers.* It should be noted, in passing, that the textbooks misinterpret the complaints of Burton and Prynne by associating them too closely with Bastwick's lavatory-language attack on the pomp and tyranny of bishops in his *Litany* (1637). Burton and Prynne were not de-

---

* At the beginning of his reign, James I extended the normal fast days of the Church of England to include every Wednesday of the year. Wednesdays and Fridays had for centuries been the regular fast days of the Roman Catholic and Greek Orthodox Churches. In England, the newly appointed day of abstinence and prayer coincided with the Puritan habit of supporting (privately and corporately) lectureships for preachers who would preach both on Sunday and in the mid-week. The Wednesday fast and the mid-week lecture, or sermon, became a mainstay of Puritan worship in the following decades. Intentionally or no, James's grant was a great fillip to Puritanism.

manding a Presbyterian system of Church government; rather, they were protesting, specifically, the innovations and censorship of the new *Book of Fasts,* and, more generally, the growing prevalence of ceremonialism—at which point they overlapped with Bastwick. Not one authority mentions the 1636 proclamation, in my view such an important factor in the Puritans' alarm. Before the proclamation, some of the "innovations" to which the Puritans objected had been merely individual preferences, such as holding episcopacy *jure divino* (the first complaint of the Root and Branch Petition) and bowing to the altar. Now, however, there were other innovations—the omission of a collect, failure to mention Elizabeth in prayer—that had received official sanction.

Only in the context of the advancing tide of ritualism can the Puritans' distress be fully understood. Given their conviction that ritualism implied Romanism, and that Arminians (in Puritan eyes no better than thinly disguised Papists) were now controlling the government, the pricks were taken to be thrusts of the knife.

Ritualism had advanced with the late Elizabethan Arminians like Andrewes and Cosin. After Abbot's lax primacy (and Abbot, stuck between Bancroft and Laud, was more important for what he did not do than for what he did), Arminianism became Canterbury's norm. What had first been individual practice was consolidated as ecclesiastical policy by the Metropolitan Visitation of 1635. And in 1636, with the royal visitation of Oxford, the Arminianism of the administration was published to the world. Not only was the occasion marked by plays (Prynne's bane) and feasting, but the clergy had decorated their chapels with "church work of the best kind they could get from the other side." "Where the east end admits not glass, excellent pictures, large and great . . . of the birth, passion, resurrection and ascension of our blessed Saviour; all their communion tables fairly covered with rich carpets, hung some of them with good hangings."[57] According to Bastwick, the Church was "as full of ceremonies as dog is full of fleas," and "the multitude of trumperies" recently introduced had destroyed the substance of religion.[58]

Both at the Censure of Bastwick, Burton, and Prynne, and at his own trial, Laud answered the Puritans' charges of innovation calmly and persuasively. There had been alterations, he admitted, but royal authority backed them all. The omission of prayers for the Navy befitted new circumstances, since the Navy was not then engaged in war; the change to "at the name of Jesus" was consistent with the Queen's Injunctions of 1559 (Art. 52); bowing to the altar belonged to the category of aesthetic devotional improvements, Laud's "beauty of holiness"; and the altar railed in the east end was but a tidy change in the interests of uniformity, since this was its position in Queen Elizabeth's chapel, and in all cathedrals. Laud was merely making "parish churches . . . conformable to the Cathedral and mother churches, rather than the cathedrals to them."[59] All alterations, he argued, were consistent with the Book of Common Prayer and the Thirty-nine Articles.

Laud, it seems, was genuinely unable to understand what all the fuss was about. He claimed that the alterations were not intended as affronts to Puritanism. For instance, he said, the banning of sermons in London on the Wednesday fast was designed to prevent people from gathering where the plague was raging; tradition, not Popery, had determined the keeping of Wednesdays for weekly fasting. Laud may have been sincere; he was certainly both thoughtless and tactless.

But then Laud found Puritan fears of his Popery incomprehensible and absurd—an indication, perhaps, of how widely separated the two parties had become. Puritans were being oversensitive to smell Romanism in every ceremonial; they were wrong to see idolatry in signs of reverence toward the altar, paranoidal to discover adoration of the elements in kneeling to receive. They simply failed to grasp the full extent of Anglicans' expectations; they could not accept devotionalism as a harmless outlet for the Anglican concentration on the sacraments. Equally, Laud had no understanding of Puritanism's lesser vision, or patience with its fears. Puritan suspicions, however, cannot be dismissed out of hand; for ultimately the Puritans were right. Their mistake was to attach Popery to the trappings of religion rather than to a deeper source. Anglicanism's view of the sacraments, as providing the only continuous and effective means to heaven, was a Roman Catholic carry-over. And though Anglicanism was unequivocally Protestant in its overt doctrine, its dynamic expectations of grace through the sacraments were thoroughly traditional.*

Eschatology

Eschatology means the doctrine of last things: death, resurrection, immortality, judgment, the fate of the world, Christ's second advent, and the future state. Here, however, we shall consider only those aspects of the subject that were conceived differently by Anglican and Puritan: in particular, their understandings of judgment and joy.

According to current opinion, the Puritans expected unremitting severity on Judgment Day, whereas Anglicans looked forward to leniency. This is an oversimplification, but with certain qualifications the antithesis holds. Two commentaries may be taken as representative of the two traditions: namely, John Pearson's *Exposition of the Creed* (1659) and William Perkins' *Of the Creed* (1600). To compare these two works on the clause "from thence He shall come to judge the quick and the dead" is not only an instructive exercise, but a fair one, since both men were predestinarians: the elect would be welcomed to Heaven and the reprobates relegated to Hell.

Despite this belief, the Anglican Pearson held a view of judgment that mitigated the severity of the double decree: "We should believe that Christ shall sit upon the throne, that our Redeemer shall be our Judge, that we shall receive our sentence not according to the rigour of the Law, but the mildness and mercies of the Gospel; and then we may look upon not only the

---

* Further evidence of Anglicanism's dynamic view of the sacraments is probably provided by the fact that marriage, confirmation, and burial were retained as sacramental rites, whereas Puritanism regarded marriage and burial as ordinances, and confirmation as unnecessary. Some extreme sects reduced marriage to a civil contract, and even eliminated religious rites in the burial of their dead. Puritanism, of course, chafed at the use of symbols in services that were not sacraments, as the wedding ring in marriage.

precepts but also the promises of God; whatsoever sentence in the sacred Scripture speaketh anything of hope, whatsoever text administreth anything of comfort, whatsoever argument drawn from them can breed in us any assurance, we may confidently make use of them all in reference to the Judgement to come, because by that Gospel which contains them all shall we be judged. . . . He which is judge is also our Advocate; and who shall condemn us, if he shall pass the sentence upon us, who maketh intercession for us."[60]

Now, obviously, Pearson's sense of Christ's mercy and intercession sits uneasily with his realization of the damnation of the non-elect. Indeed, because we have been taught to regard predestination as a dominating doctrine, we seem to be faced with a gross inconsistency. If, however, we reduce the doctrine of predestination to its proper proportions, an inconsistency remains, but not a gross one. Pearson's position, and it was the position of that rigid predestinarian Whitgift, becomes, "Yes, the damned will be damned, but all may expect mercy far beyond their just deserts."

At this point we ask: How could mercy operate except to save? Anglicanism solved the problem by assuming there was a scale, or gradation, of torments in Hell. A man could be reprobated and yet receive a lighter sentence than he deserved, than had been predetermined for him. "It is absolutely necessary," wrote Pearson, "to believe that a just and exact retribution is defined, that a due and proportionable dispensation of rewards and punishments is reserved to another world."[61] On the whole, Anglicans were chary of specifying precisely what the levels of torments were, though Latimer believed in "three degrees of punishment"; "for the greater the sin is, the greater is the punishment in hell."[62] James Ussher's *Principles of Christian Religion* likewise presupposed a proportion between punishment and crime.[63] The doctrine was standard Augustinianism, for according to Augustine God could "interpose some little respite," so that in Hell "some will have a more tolerable burden of misery than others."[64] Once this was assumed, Anglicans were able to reconcile God's mercy with the fact of non-election: for though the reprobate might not know God, God could still lessen the burden of his affliction. In Hell, mercy was mingled with justice. Though Anglicans categorically denied the existence of Purgatory, one cannot help wondering whether a trace of the Roman Catholic idea did not remain in these gradated punishments.

Of course, Arminian theology raised no barriers to an eschatology of felicity, since all were predisposed to grace by God's action from the outset, and only the obstinate and perverse—the self-condemned—willed their own destruction.

For non-Arminian Anglicans like Pearson and Ussher, or Whitgift and Jewel, the difficulty of reconciling prevenient reprobation with God's mercy was lessened by their view of sacrament. Since they regarded the sacraments as vitally effective spiritual media, all contrite partakers in the sacrament were, if not saved, at least touched by grace. Hence all members of the visible Church could expect leniency, though not all would be saved. The Anglican approach to the sacraments dulled the sense of impending doom, and bolstered the hope of final beatitude. Indeed, Arminianism in England may well have developed directly from an expanded conception of the grace that comes with the sacraments (and the correlative eschatology of contentment); for though it is not conclusive, it is certainly significant that Andrewes—an Arminian independent of Arminius—and all the Jacobean Arminians sustained the same high notion of sacramental grace. Probably this is a question of theological genealogy rather than history, so we shall not pursue it. The main point is that an expectation of universal mercy was perfectly consistent with Anglicanism's dynamic view of the sacraments; and Anglican eschatology did not necessarily clash with the belief in predetermined reprobation, so long as that belief was allotted minor importance.

The Puritans' doctrine of destiny raised as many problems as the Anglicans'. Perkins depicted Christ as a Judge who was unbendingly just, meticulously thorough, in His arraignment of sin. The unrighteous would be cast into a place of unspeakable torment, while the righteous would see God, as He had foreknown.[65] An aura of impending disaster pervaded Perkins' treatment of the sinner's fate, an aura that spread beyond Puritanism into the philosophies of moderate Separatists, though not to the millenarians. Bunyan's autobiographical *Grace Abounding to the Chief of Sinners* (1666) displays it rather naïvely. Being convinced of sin, Bunyan trembled for his life. He had taken great delight in ringing the church bells, but "began to think 'how if one of the bells should fall,'" and thereafter stood prudently at the door. "Then it came into my head, 'how if the steeple should fall,'" which forced him to flee altogether. Man's destiny was destruction, not mercy, unless God saved him.

In Puritanism, however, it is not the fate of the unrighteous that raises a problem, but the status of the saved: must they, too, harbor the sense of suffering and doom? Yes, answered Perkins, at least for the world at large; for the fate of their unchosen brethren must always hang before them. Moreover, on Judgment Day, they themselves would be submitted to a vigorous cross-examination. God had tabulated everyone's secret thoughts and actions in His mind, so that "when we shall stand before the judgement seat of Christ, he then knowing all things in his eternal court, shall reveal unto every man in his own particular sins, whether they were in thought, word or deed, and then also by his mighty power he shall so touch men's consciences, that they shall afresh remember what they have done."[66] Even for the sheep, though more for the goats, judgment would prove a stern ordeal. Calvin was the immediate source of this picture; commenting on *Jude,* he had stressed that "the vengeance suspended over the wicked ought to keep the elect in fear and watchfulness."[67] In different degrees, both the righteous and the unrighteous were destined to live out their lives in fear.

Puritanism's eschatology, like Anglicanism's, created a tension of doctrines; but again it would be going too far to call it a real conflict. The knowledge of the final trial did not damage the certainty of assurance; for it was not fear of damnation that assailed the elect, but fear of penultimate wrath, fear of the account to be rendered at the inevitable stock-taking of the talents God had given them. A tension was inescapable: the believer ought to be disquieted about his own worthiness, yet never doubt God's intentions. "When we say that faith must be certain and secure, we certainly speak not of an assurance which is never affected by doubt, nor a security which anxiety never assails, we rather maintain that believers have a perpetual struggle with their own distrust, and are thus far from thinking that their consciences possess a placid quiet, uninterrupted by perturbation. On the other hand, whatever be the mode in which they are assailed, we deny that they fall off and abandon that sure confidence which they have formed in the mercy of God."[68] Calvin's explanation denies the existence of a contradiction, but does not resolve the tension. Indeed, a glaring inconsistency would develop if he did, for the eschatology of impending doom follows from a belief in man's total depravity, whereas the assurance of faith proceeds from the sovereignty of God; and the one was the obverse of the other.

Anglicanism tended toward universalism by generalizing its hopes of intercession. Universalism, however, was a tendency and not a fact, since Anglicans never forgot that a man would be required to account for his sins. John Donne, most morbid of Anglicans, described the Day of Judgment in terms so bleak that he could well be suspected of Puritanism, were no concessions made for poetic imagination.[69] Yet it is clear that the sense of joy overwhelmed his desperation: "Joy is the blessedness of the next life, but the entering, the inchoation is afforded here. . . . So the true joy of a good soul in this world is the very joy of Heaven; and we go thither not that being without joy, we might have joy infused into us, but that Christ says, 'Our joy might be full,' perfected, sealed with an everlastingness. . . . So in the agonies of Death, in the anguish of that dissolution, in the sorrows of that valediction, in the irreversibleness of that transmigration, I shall have a joy, which shall no more evaporate, than my soul shall evaporate, A joy; that shall pass up, and put on a more glorious garment above, and be joy superinvested in glory. Amen."[70]

The dispositions of men's minds cannot be categorized. Donne's forebodings of destruction suggest Puritanism; yet, ultimately, both particular passages, and all his statements, belie that suspicion. To take an example from the other side, there are moments of personal ecstasy in Baxter's *The Saints Everlasting Rest*; yet on the whole his eschatology is austere. By and large, then, Anglicanism tended toward universalism by expecting universal mercy: though not all could expect salvation, all would be treated with leniency. Puritanism, on the other hand, moved in the opposite direction: some were saved, but all had to undergo the severity of judgment. No blanket conclusions can be given, since Anglicanism was not universalistic, neither did Puritanism expect universal reprobation. Furthermore, the ideas about the Last Judgment were less matters of dogma than dispositions of mind. Nevertheless, if we keep these difficulties and reservations in view, we may yet characterize the two eschatologies as mercy versus impartial justice, joy versus condemnation, and subjective optimism versus an objective pessimism.

In character, the books of the Prophets Deutero-Isaiah and Jeremiah represent the Anglican and Puritan attitudes: one found serenity in contemplating the gracious promises of God; the other found life's purpose in lamenting the sins of the children of Israel, and warning the unrepentant that eternal disaster lay ahead.

Chapter 4 Doctrine and Ethics

Men in all ages have lied and cheated, fed upon vanity, exploited their fellows, hated, conspired, lived in sloth, cursed their day, blasphemed against God, or slept beyond the marriage bed. The strictures of the Church have never availed to stop, though perhaps they have sometimes stemmed, the incessant flow of sin. Every cynic knows that even those who preach the highest standards conveniently forget them from time to time. Yet despite the deficiencies of practice, we may take the social teachings of the Church in this period as the norms of respectability: prelates and preachers both created and reflected the moral standards of their day; they had far more influence than nowadays. In some measure, this may atone for the fact that we shall be dealing less with what was, than with what could and ought to have been in the eyes of those who were most concerned. Moreover, this inquiry is not intended to cover every aspect of Puritan and Anglican ethics; I am interested primarily in the effect of doctrine upon ethics, not in ethics themselves.

In their common Protestant tradition, both Anglican and Puritan claimed that good works were the fruit of the indwelling of the Holy Spirit. Works, as such, were without merit unless the heart and the intentions had first been purified by grace.[1] Yet beyond this broad and important similarity were many differences.

These differences were born of dissimilar theological emphases. Anglicanism taught an idealistic and prescriptive form of morality that derived from its doctrines of man, grace, and nature, its view of the sacraments, and its eschatology. Man was depraved, certainly—for Anglicans never doubted the doctrine of original sin—but he was also rational up to a point, and beyond salvation could be further perfected by gifts of grace dispensed by the Church through ministrations of the sacraments. Indeed, in the Anglicans' dynamic view, the sacraments could provide the grace necessary for perfection. "Our Saviour calleth his servants from the imitation of all others, and willeth them to set him before their eyes as a perfect pattern and absolute example" reads a handbook of Anglican piety.[2] An imitation of Christ was conceivable, of course, only after an infusion of the Holy Spirit. In *A Progress of Piety* (1596), John Norden wrote: "Sanctify me within and without: wash me and I shall be whiter than snow"; his prayer was based on the confidence "that he will sanctify us within; that he will make our whole lump holy, the root and the branches holy. If our heart be pure, all our actions will likewise be pure."[3] Anglicanism did not really expect to live Christ-like, but thought it was possible.

Reinhold Niebuhr has associated this perfectionist trait with nonconformity, and it is true that some dissenting sects—like the Family of Love, to mention an extreme—were perfectionists; their sources of theological inspiration, however, were different from those that informed Anglicanism.[4] Professor Niebuhr found the characteristic in the writings of John Wesley in the eighteenth century, but Wesley had learned it as an Anglican, and imported it into modern nonconformity from there. Wesley's debate with the German Count Zinzendorf reflects the seventeenth-century split between Anglican and Puritan. Zinzendorf: "I acknowledge no inherent perfection in this life. This is the error of errors. I pursue it through the whole world with fire and the sword. Christ is our sole perfection. Whoever follows inherent perfection denies Christ." Wesley: "[But] I truly believe that the spirit of Christ works this perfection in true Christians."[5] Wesley's trust restated the theme of George Herbert's well-known poem *The Elixir,* which enjoined men to realize the fullness of perfection through dedication:

> Not rudely as a beast,
> To runne into an action;
> But still to make Thee pre-possest,
> And give it [its] perfection.

.   .   .

This is the famous stone
That turneth all to gold;
For that which God doth touch and own
Cannot for less be told.[6]

Not only was Anglicanism encouraged by doctrine to pitch its
ethics high, but it was less prone than Puritanism to formulate
an ethic for a particular situation; yet paradoxically, or perhaps
inevitably, its prescripts were open to temperate and elastic interpretation. Like Puritanism, Anglicanism realized that sin was
bound to recur, yet it did not consider a lapse, or an evil deed, as
heinous an offense as Puritanism did. This is not to argue that
Anglicanism was lax, merely laxer than Puritanism. Anglicans
could admit flexibility because they believed that after repentance the sacrament was fully able to restore a sinner to a state of
grace, and also because their eschatology of mercy placed the
wrongdoer under a lighter burden than the Puritan expectation
of Divine vengeance. This eschatology stressing Christ's media-
tion by no means licensed sin, but it did allow a backslider to fall
short of his obligations without putting his peace of mind in
jeopardy. It used kindness rather than severity as the incentive to
good behavior. John Woolten's *Christian Manual* (1576) exudes
this spirit of gentleness: "Surely he that calleth to mind, that he
is the son and heir of God, and the brother and fellow-heir of
Jesus Christ, will repress sin, and stay himself from wickedness,
not so much for fear of the last day and the torments of hell, as
lest he should offend and displease so loving a father."[7]

Relatively, and it is of course a matter of degree, Puritan ethics
were more pragmatic and worldly, an orientation suggested by
their doctrine of man and their vision of the dialectical relationship between the spheres of grace and nature. The principle of
absolute depravity guided Puritanism toward pragmatism by for-
bidding all utopian aspirations. Man was flesh, and even though
the Spirit predominated, the corruption of the flesh would never
be completely overcome in this life. Perfection was therefore un-
attainable. Moreover, grace was locked in a struggle with nature,
ultimately sure of victory but temporarily beset by powerful op-

position. As grace came to grips with nature, so Puritan ethics came to grips with the world, taking stock of its ways in order to subject them to the ways of righteousness.

But, like Anglicanism, Puritanism was paradoxical; for the element of worldliness in it was combined, and possibly over-shadowed, by an intense combativeness, which, also, can be traced to doctrine. The macrocosmic struggle of grace and na-ture worked in the individual in microcosm. Grace warred with sin in the believer's soul, so that as he came to understand his spiritual estate, he was compelled to join in the universal battle between sin and grace, fallen man and God. Activism was en-couraged, too, by the Puritans' conviction of strict accountability at the Last Judgment. Jeremiah once lamented of Jerusalem, "Her filthiness is in her skirts; she remembereth not her last end; therefore she came down wonderfully."[8] So long as a Puritan re-membered his last end, and that of his fellows, he could "not cease from mental strife," and he would not fall down wonder-fully. Further, as we have seen, the emphasis upon God's sover-eignty, when it was coupled with joy for His work of grace in the chosen person, far from instilling passive and stoic accept-ance, encouraged the Puritan to use every opportunity to glorify his Maker. Finally, the Puritan idea of the spirituality (and there-fore the separateness) of the Church in the world, when it was added to the primary expectation of grace through gospel con-frontation rather than through the sacraments, made the Puri-tans tireless ambassadors for Christ. All these beliefs reinforced Puritanism's combative and activist urge.

Activism, indeed, has become the hallmark of Puritanism. The fellow is anonymous who swore that he would rather have a troop of horse descend upon him than one lone Puritan con-vinced that he was right. John Downame's work *The Christian Warfare* was aptly named. Schoolboys, I suppose, still memorize Milton's "I cannot praise a fugitive and cloistered virtue," and savor its bellicose tone as much as its language.[9] To this day, the plain-spoken quality of the Separatist's hymn has its Puritan admirers:

Who would true valour see,
Let him come hither;
One here will constant be,
Come wind come weather;
There's no discouragement
Shall make him once relent
His first avowed intent
To be a pilgrim.

.   .   .

Hobgoblin nor foul fiend
Can daunt his spirit;
He knows he at the end
Shall life inherit.
Then fancies flee away;
He'll fear not what men say;
He'll labour night and day
To be a pilgrim.[10]

If, in the formulation, Puritan ethics were comparatively worldly and pragmatic, in their application they were disconcertingly astringent and assertive.

A conspicuous example of the relative laxity of Anglican morality, and of its energetic Puritan counterpart, occurred in the chronic problem of pluralism. In part, this resulted from the Church's poverty. But we cannot attribute the blame to poverty alone when we recall the considerable sums that the Puritan Feoffees for Impropriations managed to raise.* Rather, we must look to the ingrained ethical temper of Anglicanism. The Puritans might have succeeded in surmounting the obstacles, and they did make headway against the abuse during the Interregnum.[11] Anglicanism never seriously tackled the problem. According to one estimate, in 1603 some 2,400 benefices were being held by 1,000 pastors.[12]

---

* The institution of the Feoffees for Impropriations (described by the Root and Branch Petition as "that godly design . . . sugared with many great gifts of sundry well-affected persons") was introduced by the Puritans in 1625. The chief aims of the Feoffees were to buy up patrons' rights—i.e., their right to present a man to a benefice—and to provide for Puritan preachers. For further details see Isabel M. Calder, ed., *Activities of the Puritan Faction of the Church of England, 1625–33* (London, 1957); Isabel M. Calder, "A 17th Century Attempt to Purify the Anglican Church," *American Historical Review*, LIII (1948), 760–75; and Ethyn W. Kirby, "The Lay Feoffees," *Journal of Modern History*, XIV (1942), 1–25.

The record of Puritan attempts at reform was long and frustrating. The remedial bills introduced into Parliament in 1584, 1589, 1601, 1610, 1621, 1624, and 1625 were defeated. Both the Millenary Petition (Sec. 3) and the Root and Branch Petition (Sec. 20) protested the evil.[13] Much earlier, when Cartwright had supported the attack of the First Admonition upon the practice, Whitgift's reply effectively illustrated the dualism of the Anglican attitude, if it did not effectively silence the criticism. "I do not allow such as covetously 'join living to living' of what kind of men soever they be. . . . But I see no cause why one good and diligent pastor may not rather be credited with more flocks, than a slothful, unskillful, or negligent one."[14] Covetousness was abhorred, but pluralism countenanced. Christopher Hill's comment on the Canon of 1604, which permitted pluralism within a thirty-mile compass provided a curate was in place, confirms the dualism of Anglican practice: "By limiting pluralism," he concludes, "this canon in a sense legitimated it."[15]

On the question of civil obedience, however, Anglicans displayed the other aspect of their ethic. The tenth of the Homilies of 1547, which concerns "Good Order and Obedience," sets the tone for subsequent thought. One foot of its argument was the utilitarian virtue of an orderly creation, a case that Shakespeare states with such force in *Troilus and Cressida* (I, iii):

> Take but degree away, untune that string,
> And, hark! what discord follows . . .

The other foot of the argument rested upon the Scriptures. Using St. Peter's command that servants be obedient, the homily exhorts congregations to be "patient and of the suffering kind," even toward an evil rule.[16] The Anglican Edwin Sandys, who was a man of moderate views in both religion and politics, drew the same lesson from Scripture: "One reason why every soul should be in subjection to the higher power is because whosoever resisteth the ordinance of God provoketh the judgement of God against himself. If God for thy sin set a wanton, an hypocrite, yea, or an infidel over thee, thou must obey that wanton, that hypocrite, and that Infidel, and not rebel against him."[17] As

Hooker shows, Elizabethan Anglicans managed to reconcile an ethic of absolute obedience with a theory of monarchy by consent.[18]

By the seventeenth century, however, the ethic of absolute obedience had been linked to an absolutist theory of government. Along with the legal and historical arguments that he had elaborated in *The True Law of Free Monarchies* (1598), James I used both the Scriptures and homely analogues of family and bodily structures to establish his Divine ordination and the absolute duty of obedience. In 1609 he told Parliament that "the State of MONARCHY is the supremest thing upon earth: for Kings are not only GOD's lieutenants upon earth, and sit upon GOD's throne, but even by God himself they are called Gods. . . . In the Scriptures Kings are called Gods. . . . Kings are also compared to Fathers of families: For a King is truly *parens patriae*, the politic father of his people. And lastly kings are compared to the head of this Microcosm of the body of a man."[19] In no circumstances did subjects have the right to rebel, not even in order to resist "the deadly poison of tyranny."[20]

Understandably, James was fertile in his own defense. Yet we should not regard his pleading as ridiculous:[21] he was merely making explicit some of the commonplaces of his day. Robert Filmer later expanded James's notion of the King as *parens patriae* in his *Patriarcha* (1680), and a useful summary of Filmer's arguments closes his *Observations Touching Forms of Governments* (1679): "1. That there is no form of government but monarchy only. 2. That there is no monarchy, but paternal. 3. That there is no paternal monarchy, but absolute or arbitrary."[22] Here obedience was enjoined to an extreme constitutional theory; but whatever the Anglicans' understanding of sovereignty, whether moderate or extreme, their ethic remained an unqualified and absolute prescription.

Under James II, Anglicans were forced into a quandary by bare political and religious facts; for James was a Catholic, and a Catholic succession seemed imminent. It caused Anglicans some anguish to give way to a new order that decreed absolute obedience to a Providence who had plainly anointed William of Orange.[23] The sharpness of the dilemma facing the Church in

1688 bears witness to the strength of its teaching beforehand. And to understand the weight of the old teaching makes Cranmer's end more poignant: he was not simply wavering, under stress, between religious principle and physical weakness; he was torn between conviction and conviction, one doctrine and another.[24]

Right from the beginning, Puritanism attached a qualification to the ethic of strict civil obedience, and was prepared to hammer out the path of duty in the light of its first principle of obedience to God. In other words, I suggest that the moral expediency of Puritanism derived, at least in part, from doctrine. This, of course, does not invalidate the claim that Puritan ethics were shaped by political circumstances. Obviously they were. I suggest merely that a pliable ethic followed after a pliable doctrine, and not the other way about—a suggestion that is strengthened by the fact that Calvin had cast his system before he entered Geneva, where the situation was so appropriate for it. Anglicanism, on the other hand, failed to rethink its teachings under the trauma of Mary Tudor's reversion to Catholicism, an indication (if my theory is correct) of a less pliable doctrine.

Be this as it may, Calvin, in the first edition of his *Institutes,* had allowed the people's magistrates (i.e., representatives) the right to resist. He concluded his work with the thought that "we ought to obey God rather than man (Acts v. 29)";[25] and in the last aphorism of his *Book of Aphorisms* he justified a form (and also limited the instruments) of civil disobedience: "The obedience enjoined on subjects does not prevent the interference of any popular Magistrates whose office is to restrain tyrants and protect the liberty of the people. Our obedience to Magistrates ought to be such that the obedience we owe to the King of Kings shall remain entire and unimpaired."[26] One naturally wonders what stimulated Calvin to provide this opening and this justification for resistance. According to one interpretation, he was developing an idea of Zwingli's; according to another, he was following a suggestion of Bucer's, and giving it historic application in Geneva. Both explanations may be right, or perhaps Calvin arrived at the idea independently.[27]

The Puritans adopted Calvin's idea, though no theory of positive resistance sprang from them under Elizabeth. At least they recognized the practical difficulty in the way of the Anglican ideal—that the wills of earthly and heavenly crowns might clash —and grappled with it. Perkins, in *A Treatise of Conscience* (1596), paused at the critical point in the discussion of obedience: "Magistracy indeed is an ordinance of God to whom we owe subjection, but how far subjection is due, there is the question." How, indeed, should the Christian act if a monarch contravened God's will? "If it shall fall out that men's law be made of things that are evil and forbidden by God, then is there no bond of concience at all; but contrariwise men are bound in concience not to obey."[28] A similar reservation was contained in Henry Smith's statement that the first lesson was to fear God, and the next to honor the King; that men should obey for conscience and not against it.[29] In words as well as in deeds the Puritans kept the door ajar for possible defiance, nominating as the guardians of justice both "prophets" and popular representatives.[30]

As circumstances changed, provision for possible resistance became a proclamation of positive duty—at least for the radicals in the Civil War, who saw themselves as obliged to disobey an arbitrary and unrighteous monarch. This obligation was stated with varying degrees of force. John Eliot, in *De Jure Maiestatis* (1631), conceded surprisingly large powers to the monarch, but nevertheless claimed that a king was bound "so far forth as the public good and the laws of God and nature do require."[31] These few words allowed a wealth of interpretation, including the justification for Eliot's disobedience. Samuel Rutherford's *Lex Rex* (1644) is a more fully developed plea for opposition, but not nearly so strident as Milton's *Tenure of Kings and Magistrates* (1649). Milton quoted earlier opinion with approval: "When Kings or Rulers become blasphemers of God, . . . they ought no more to be accounted Kings or lawful Magistrates, but as private men to be examined, accused, Condemned and punished by the law of God."[32] The movement in England from the hesitant reservations about the duty of obedience to the violent clamors of theorists in the Civil War illustrates the pliability within the Puritans' ethic: their standards could be and were developed in the light of new situations and new events. Our concern, however, is not so much to analyze the changes as to draw attention to the inherent pragmatism of the Puritan ethic, and therein to show its variance from the Anglican norm.

In the sense that a Christian today would have difficulty squaring his principles with doctrinaire Marxism, theology could be said to set boundaries, or negative limits, upon political attitudes. The Puritans' view of the Church rendered both formal hierarchy and the royal supremacy in religious matters superfluous. Puritanism was thus both logically and actually predisposed to limit some of the prerogatives of the Crown. Similarly, in theory, Separatism would have set even greater limitations on the Crown; but many Separatists (like Bunyan or Fox), also for religious reasons, were essentially apolitical. Rarely did theology dictate the formal content of a political ideology, the Fifth Monarchists being an exception. In the English Civil War, neither the Presbyterians nor the Independents were impelled to republicanism. They preferred to limit rather than destroy the prerogatives of the Crown. Both could have retained Kingship, though not as Charles understood it. Cromwell, despite his disagreements with the Presbyterians, leaned toward monarchy almost as much as they. He wanted a government "somewhat with monarchical power in it,"[33] a wish that almost provided a basis for settlement with the Presbyterians during the Protectorate. It stands, however, that Puritanism felt comfortable only with a limited monarchy; but just how limited theology did not decree.

Of late, special attention has been devoted to the Puritans' use of the concept of the covenant. Indeed, according to Leonard J. Trinterud, the development of Puritanism can be traced to its covenant theology. He sharply distinguishes a mutual covenant idea, which he finds indigenous to England and the Rhineland, from Calvin's unilateral understanding of God's relationship to man. On this basis, "the origins and development of the Puritan synthesis must be traced along the lines of the rise and career of this [mutual] covenant notion. This notion in its secular form was pre-Reformation in English thought and life. The theological formulation of the covenant appeared first in English literature with Tyndale." "Wherever one turns in an examination of the Puritanism of this period he finds the covenant-contract notion."[34] While Professor Trinterud's argument is refreshing, it remains unconvincing for a number of reasons.

First, the distinction between Calvin's unilateral theory and Tyndale's reciprocal one has been too sharply drawn. Tyndale's covenant idea certainly placed a heavy burden of good behavior upon the individual. But Calvin did not disoblige man from the duty of trying to fulfill the law, or of trying to live righteously, even at those times when he was at pains to show, against the Romans, that man could perform nothing worthy of evoking a reciprocal promise from God. Thus, in the *Institutes,* he wrote: "Paul by the word Law frequently intends the rule of a righteous life, in which God requires of us what we owe to him, affording us no hope of life, unless we fulfil every part of it." And again: "All those persons, from the beginning of the world, whom God has adopted into the society of his people, have been federally connected with him by the same doctrines which are now in force among us."[35] Finally, in discussing God's covenant with Abraham, Calvin asserted that "the covenant of God with Abram had two parts. The first was a declaration of gratuitous love. . . . But the other was an exhortation to the sincere endeavour to cultivate righteousness."[36] The point may seem picayune, for Trinterud is undoubtedly correct to stress the greater mutuality assumed in Tyndale's covenant; but at the same time, we should remember that reciprocity was not altogether absent in Calvin.

Second, I do not believe that the Puritan concept of the covenant can be conclusively linked with Tyndale. Tyndale believed that God could and might withdraw from the contract, that God's part was dependent upon man's good behavior.[37] That God could renege was a presumption abhorrent to English Puritanism, and this, to my mind, establishes the non-Tyndalistic nature of Puritan thought on the subject. Indeed, the Puritan position was nearer to Calvin's. Calvin's sense of God's part in the covenant was the opposite of Tyndale's: God's promises were unconditional, from everlasting unto everlasting; He would never withdraw them (though He might impose salutary punishments), and His promises were entirely gratuitous.[38] John Preston, whom Perry Miller quotes in this connection, was staunchly Calvinistic.[39] In *The Doctrine of the Saints' Infirmities* (1630), Preston wrote: "So long as a man is in the covenant, his infirmities cannot cut him off from God's mercy. Now it is certain, we may have many infirmities, and the covenant remain unbroken: for every sin doth not break the covenant."[40] Some sins, such as adultery, were evidence that a man had probably never been in the covenant. "God," said Preston, "cannot forget his covenant."[41] Or, in another work, Preston asserted that "if ever thou art in the covenant with God, and hast this seal in thy soul, that there is a change wrought in thee by the covenant, and thy election is sure, be then sure also God will never alter it, for he is unchangeable."[42] Professor Miller's findings about the covenant should not be accepted too uncritically, but in this particular respect his emphasis on Calvinism is valuable. Certainly, Puritanism did not share Tyndale's view that God's promises were conditional.

Third, covenant theology does not seem to loom so large in English Puritan thought as has been suggested.[43] As a verbal shorthand, to represent the substance of the Gospel—God's love, Christ's atonement, and the sinner's redemption—the word covenant is used; but this usage in the sense of "the testament" does not carry Tyndale's meaning of a particular contractual bond between creature and Creator.[44] According to Trinterud, Cartwright and Dudley Fenner were the leading exponents of the concept; however, there is little stress upon it in Cartwright, and although Fenner develops a bold theory of political contract in his *Sacra Theologica* (1585), his understanding of the theological contract in this and in his other doctrinal writings is of the Calvinist kind—the free promises of the covenant of John Cotton.[45] Moreover, according to Knappen, Fenner's work "had no great popularity or influence."[46]

Far from finding covenant theology at every turn, I had to look for it. Possibly there has been some confusion of the secular and the theological principles. If so, the secular, medieval theory of government by consent is quite inadequate as a means of differentiation between Anglican and Puritan; for, as R. W. K. Hinton points out, the mixed or mutual constitutional theory was common to most Elizabethans.[47] The constitutional and the theological theories cannot be equated.

True, a covenant idea did rise to prominence in the seventeenth century, with those who joined together to journey to New England and—most strikingly—with the adherents of the National Covenant (1638) and the Solemn League and Covenant (1643) in Scotland. We need not run, with Champlin Burrage, to the Continental Anabaptists for the origin of the idea.[48] The Bible was nearer to hand; it provided covenants of mutual interest (Abraham and Abimelech) and of mutual love (David and Jonathan) that were appropriate to the needs of the moment. These contracts, however, were between man and man rather than God and man. As Milton realized, they belonged to the realm of nature: "No understanding man can be ignorant that Covenants are ever made according to the present state of persons and of things."[49] They were not the same as the Covenant of God with Abraham or Moses, or the new covenant in Christ's blood with the true believers. They were earthbound, devotional, and tactical—compacts made for mutual protection against external dangers, compacts, even, of defiance.[50] They were adjuncts to the pragmatic and combative qualities of Puritanism. Their origin was Biblical, and their shape, naturally, consistent with the participative and congregational impulse of Puritan churchmanship.

Finally, even if the covenant were a central dogma, it would remain methodologically unconvincing to fasten the origins of Puritanism on the pedigree of one idea alone.

Yet although Tyndale's conditional covenant theology was foreign to the main body of Puritans, it does crop up in the works of the Separatist Robert Browne.[51] Indeed, Separatism seems its natural home, for the Church in this kind of covenant requires to be composed only of the good, those voluntarily dedicated to

Christ. And from this assumption follows the quasi-Donatist nature of Separatism's theology. Trinterud may have hit upon a characteristic that distinguishes Separatists from other Puritans, rather than a quality common to all Puritanism.

My researches, then, have confirmed the traditional conclusion that Calvin, while drawing on a voluminous store of Protestant thought (in particular Zwingli's principle of *scriptura sola*), introduced elements that were sufficiently novel in themselves to found a separate "school." And from Geneva his influence spread to England, where it proved compatible with many indigenous and imported strains, and incompatible with others. Hopefully, it is possible to hold this conclusion and still give credit to those early pre-Reformers like Tyndale and Frith, and before them Wycliffe and the Lollards, who prepared the English for the Reformation and for Protestantism in general.

To argue, as I have done, that Anglican and Puritan ethics were amalgams of opposites—to cite Anglican laxness and Puritan rigor in one case, then Anglican perfectionism and Puritan opportunism in another—is to oversimplify matters. Various ethical balances were possible. The more devout of the Anglican clergy and laity presumably stayed close to the high ideals of their religion, as the more earnest Puritans would wrestle rather than run with the world. But obviously great variations of behavior could occur between the ethical extremes, and objectively the members of one group might be morally indistinguishable from the members of the other. On one issue a fairly stable synthesis could emerge; on another there could be a wide range of teaching. To take civil disobedience as an example: Anglicanism, true to its high precepts, would not begin a revolution, but, consistent with its lenience, could acquiesce in one; Puritanism, on the other hand, could be a pillar of order or a battering ram of discontent, or both at the same time, depending upon its relationship to the seat of power. Those who see Puritanism as a revolutionary ideology and those who see it as a bulwark of conservatism are both right; they are wrong only insofar as they reject the opposite possibility.

Recent work on casuistry illustrates the ambiguities within

each creed. George Mosse, after examining the reactions of the Puritans Perkins and Ames to the idea of "reason of state," was impressed both by their acceptance of practical necessities and by the sincerity of their attempts to measure all action by the demands of godliness.[52] Jeremy Taylor, a staunch Episcopalian, was even bolder and blunter than the two Puritans in his willingness to accept political exigency, and more explicit about the need for "adjustment to changing times." By contrast, Robert Sanderson and William Sancroft, who were equally staunch Anglicans, flatly denounced all concessions to "prudence" as immoral;[53] while the moderate Thomas Fuller begged to avoid the issue altogether.[54]

It is in business affairs, however, that we see the ambivalence of Anglican and Puritan attitudes most clearly. A plethora of scholarship now exists upon the relationship of Protestantism to capitalism, much of it apparently irreconcilable, and much of it bedeviled by the basic difficulty of defining capitalism. Weber defined it as the rationalization of the acquisitive urge; Sombart as a vague yet pervasive spirit of enterprise; Fanfani as an unencumbered mentality of commercialism; and Marx as the prevalence and acceptance of market relations. The last may yet be the most useful description because the "spirit of capitalism" is not a simple entity.[55] It was at once hedonistic and ascetic (one could do what one liked with one's money so long as most of it was invested); it was more amoral than immoral; it was calculating but also intuitive, parsimonious yet prodigal when the winds seemed propitious, disciplined and also adventurous, individualistic yet frequently requiring participation in joint ventures. Capitalism could deploy a variety of talents for success, and capitalists cannot be stereotyped. This difficulty turns the pursuit of viable parallels into a chase after a greased pig.

The imaginative hypotheses of Weber and Troeltsch have been undermined by a winding procession of revisionist scholars: Sombart, Lujo Brentano, Tawney, Henri Hauser, Henri Sée, H. M. Robertson, Albert Hyma, George Harkness, Conrad Moehlmann, and André Sayous, not to mention the more recent contributors.[56] Of these, some modify and some wholly deny the existence of correlations, and there is such a proliferation of views that it is impossible to say precisely where the argument now stands. However, it lies beyond my scope to try to summarize the history of the controversy,* and I shall assume that the reader has a working acquaintance with the scholarship on the subject. We can then concentrate on the primary aim of elaborating the ethical frameworks that doctrine bequeathed to morality.

After half a century of debate, it may seem naïve to imagine that we can still light upon a synthesis of the conflicting impulses of Anglican and Puritan ethics. Yet we have the advantage of being able to restrict the discussion to England, and within this limitation some sort of synthesis—at least of the more moderate judgments of the scholars—does seem possible. Such a reconciliation, for example, would appear to corroborate by inference Biéler's strange claim that Calvinism in Geneva both retarded and stimulated capitalism.[57] Indeed, the intrinsic ambiguity of Anglican and Puritan (or Calvinist) ethics may help to explain why such sharply antithetical interpretations could have been drawn from the same evidence.

Consider usury, which, according to the contemporary definition, was an agreement made before an exchange of capital, the borrower contracting to pay the lender a fixed sum in excess of the principal. The inflexibility of the bargain, whatever the circumstances, was an integral part of usury, and it was this rigidity that Shakespeare used with such skill in *The Merchant of Venice*. Adventuring principal, making a profit after risk and some labor, hiring or letting, entering a partnership for gain and loss—these undertakings were not usurious.

Professor Tawney noticed the curious fact that the Anglican Church was consistently sterner in its prohibitions of usury than the Churches of the Continent; and recent analyses have confirmed his view.[58] Jewel's judgment of usury was magnificent for its unqualified condemnation: "Usury is a kind of lending of money [or non-fungible goods] wherein, upon a covenant and bargain; we receive again the whole principal which we

* A good deal has emerged since Ephraim Fischoff's "The Protestant Ethic and the Spirit of Capitalism: The History of a Controversy," in *Social Research*, XI (1944), 61–77.

delivered and somewhat more, for the use and occupancy of the same. . . . It is filthy gains, and a work of darkness. It is a monster in nature."[59] Less impassioned but more formidable was Thomas Wilson's *Discourse upon Usury* (1571). John Blaxton marshaled a chorus of clerics to reprove the sin;[60] and Thomas Culpepper demanded the unconditional repeal of the Act of 1571 (of which more later).[61] Consistent with the idealistic character of its ethics, Anglicanism was splendidly unwavering in its attacks upon usury right up to the Civil War.

Tawney's works remain the finest in the field, yet he appears to have exaggerated the Puritans' willingness to accept usury as lawful. The Puritan Robert Bolton was almost as unyielding in his condemnation of it as the Anglican Roger Fenton,[62] and Henry Smith was even more disapproving. He admitted that *Deuteronomy* (xxiii. 20) condoned usury if the debtor were a stranger, but pointed out that this was an extremely small category.[63] Nevertheless, even in such instances, there remains some truth in the contention that Puritanism was more prone than Anglicanism to allow the legality of certain kinds of usury. Perkins' attitude is perhaps typical:

> Question: Is it more lawful to take at some time above the principal?
> Answer: Yes surely, with these conditions: I. If a man take heed that he exact nothing but that which his debtor can get by good and lawful means. II. He may not take more than the gain, nary, not all the gain, that he must not require the principal, if his debtor be by inevitable and just casualities brought behind, and it be also plain that he could not make, no not by great diligence, any commodity of the money borrowed.[64]

Many Puritans accepted the fact of usury, but did their best to purge it of its exploitative quality. It is difficult to know which aspect of their attitude to emphasize. According to Tawney, Richard Baxter's down-to-earth understanding of commercial transactions indicated a practical moralism that developed in the earlier period of Puritan thought. Later scholars, however, claim that Baxter's moralism was restrictive, and that this was typical of his times and creed.[65] The truth may lie on both sides, in that practicality as well as a pugnacious repressiveness were fundamental to all Puritanism.

The Usury Act of 1571 is sometimes taken as a sign of the low moral standards of the times.[66] Professor Hyma mistook it for approbation of usury below 10 per cent; and he further assumed, without justification, that the Puritans were opposed to it, since he was under the impression that the earlier Act of 1552, which had prohibited usury altogether as a criminal offense, was a Puritan rather than an Anglican policy. In fact, the Act of 1571 rendered all bargains charging more than 10 per cent automatically void; moreover, reviving the Act of 1545, it imposed not only the penalty of forfeiture of three times the principal and the interest, but also fines and imprisonment as for an offense against the dignity of the Crown; and, finally, it left the offender liable to the penalties of the Ecclesiastical Law. Transactions under 10 per cent were subject to a lesser penalty—the forfeiture of the interest only—and offenders in this category were withdrawn from the jurisdiction of Ecclesiastical Law. A suitor could thus escape paying interest, and repay the principal alone, if he took the case to law. Presumably, though, he would ruin his credit, involve himself in considerable expense, and run the risk of losing the case; for, as Bolton complained, there were plenty of magistrates prepared to find grounds for upholding usurious contracts. But in no sense was the aim of the Act to fix a legal maximum of 10 per cent, or to approve usury below that limit. Rather, it permitted limited usury, *ultra vires,* offering neither the sanction nor yet the vindictive opposition of the law to low rates. In 1624 the 10 per cent line of demarcation was reduced to 8 per cent.[67]

The positions of Anglicans and Puritans cannot be gathered from what remains of the debate on the Bill. Thomas Wilson, the devout Anglican, spoke at length, delivering a barrage of learning against the Bill and condemning it in its entirety. Thomas Norton, the earnest Puritan, argued that all usury was injurious, and recommended that the proposal be rejected.[68] The majority of the House, and this must have included both Puritans and Anglicans, passed the Bill. No doubt they were comforted by the clause that castigated usury as a sin detestable to God. And perhaps they were swayed by the apparently disingenuous yet very practical considerations of Serjeant William

Lovelace, who argued that too sharp an attack on usury might increase covetousness.[69] The moral of the passage of the Bill seems to be that Anglicans and Puritans alike were capable of pliability, and of tempering the wind to the shorn lamb.

No one now would maintain that Puritanism sanctified the acquisition of wealth with a doctrine of calling or with a perversion of the doctrine of predestination. Wealth was not *prima facie* evidence of godliness: God blessed Abraham with riches, yet persecuted Job as a mark of special favor. Puritanism made a virtue neither of riches nor of poverty—and the same was true of Anglicanism. Puritanism stressed works, and perhaps calling, more than Anglicanism, but the fact that Anglicanism did not require so much soul-searching and self-immolation by conscience freed men for other affairs. In this respect Anglicanism was the less demanding religion. The Anglican view of man, moreover, cultivated self-confidence, whereas the Puritan vision inspired activity and effort.

Which characteristics agreed better with the elusive spirit of capitalism I would not venture. In the Church service and sacramental celebrations, Anglicanism was a shade more individualistic than Puritanism, the latter emphasizing congregational participation. Tawney's hint of a psychological attraction between the individualism of commerce and the religion of individualism could possibly be applied to Anglicanism;[70] and it could be argued equally well that the quality of participation went with commerce, in which case a link might be suggested with Puritanism. The questions to be settled are whether church attendance would condition a man for success in business; and whether a man's aptitude for business would lead him to prefer one faith to the other. On the one hand, Anglican pliability and Puritan pragmatism permitted capitalism; on the other, Anglican idealism and Puritan combativeness inhibited it. And, according to the evidence, the inhibiting characteristics predominated.*

If Puritanism did tend to promote capitalism, it would seem to me that Anglicanism was equally conducive to it, equally able

---

* Admittedly the evidence is one-sided, for the most articulate in each camp were also the most pious.

to provide a rationale for exploitation. Both religions, however, were uneasy with commercialism, and profiteers presumably made indifferent Christians. So long as faith was meaningful, the tensions between perfectionism and latitude, pragmatism and strictness, were more oppressive than encouraging to capitalism; and when idealism gave way to indifference, and combativeness subsided into acquiescence, then the Anglicanism and the Puritanism of *ante-bellum* England could be pronounced dead and decently buried.*

In personal and domestic matters, it is vain to generalize beyond the statement that Anglicans and Puritans together hailed marriage as an ordinance of God, and joyfully renounced the Catholic ideal of chastity for the clergy. In Hooker, Herbert, Cosin, and Fuller, there was a lingering admiration for virginity and chastity that was less marked among the Puritans.[71] In Gataker, Smith, Perkins, and Adams, there was a concentration upon such practical matters as child-rearing, the palliation of lust, and the day-to-day companionability of marriage.[72] The *nuances* of perfectionism and pragmatism, however, may be too slender to bear comment.

The use (or, as Puritans frequently thought, the abuse) of leisure was discussed in Chapter 1. There it was argued that the Puritans' rigor was related to their profoundly pessimistic view of natural man, while the Anglicans' latitude followed from their belief in some capacity for good. These doctrines were supplemented and complemented by others. The Anglicans' eschatology and their high expectation of the sacraments could and did give rise to sacerdotalism. In extreme forms, such doctrines evoked intense devotionalism, or quietistic piety. More often, they provided the believer with a spiritual comforter. "How canst thou but be pleasantly affected, O my soul, with the comfortable sense of having a God, a Saviour, and heaven of thine own" mused Bishop Hall in *The Soul's Farewell to Earth,* and

---

* When the change did occur, metaphysical and doctrinal views, as well as ethical ones, were affected. Secularism and commercialism had done much to weaken both faiths. Above all, the revolutionary achievements of science popularized a new metaphysical world-view, destroying the concepts upon which Anglican and Puritan doctrines had been based and from which they had derived their powers of persuasion.

he thanked God for "this feeling [of] complacency."[73] Puritanism did not enjoy such content. Not that it lacked assurance; but its deep-seated sense of sin inspired an urge to take hold of self and the world, and to prepare for the Kingdom of Christ.

At worst, Anglicanism was sluggish and smug; at best it was marked by a humane aspiration after Christian charity, and a gentle yet persuasive stimulus to saintliness. Meanwhile Puritanism, in degeneracy, could become canting evangelicism or self-righteous worldliness; but in its vigor it called for an all-consuming effort on the part of the individual to maintain maximum integrity in every dealing for the honor of an almighty and gracious God.

Conclusion

Richard Baxter once began a sermon with the words "Fundamentals in religion are the life of the superstructure,"[1] and most sixteenth- and seventeenth-century Christians would have agreed with him. Quite legitimately, however, modern historians have tended to bypass the doctrinal approach, preferring a more secular one. But a few scholars—particularly students of Hooker— have been struck by the doctrinal gulf separating Anglican and Puritan. A. S. P. Woodhouse, for example, noticed that Hooker's philosophy of law implied "a very different view of nature, including the natural powers of the human mind, from that entertained by his Puritan opponents."[2] Unhappily his contrast was incidental to the theme of the article, so the discussion was all too brief. Similarly, R. G. Usher's profound knowledge of both Hooker and Bancroft led him to see that Anglican and Puritan diverged on the most fundamental questions of theology—on man, the universe, God, and the Church.[3] As with Woodhouse, Usher's discussion was in the nature of an aside, but he did expand his theory to a certain extent.

Anglicanism, he argued, was raised upon a belief in the immanence of God in the world; whereas Puritanism assumed the complete separation of God from the world, the bonds of Creator and created being "hopelessly sundered." My conclusions partly agree with and partly modify Usher's, since instead of asking what man's relationship with God was, I ask what God's relationship with man was. Framed this way, the question becomes more complex. Anglicanism separated God from natural man by placing Him above human nature, while at the same time joining God to man through the activity of free justification. Divine perfection, in other words, was both contiguous with man and divided from him. God could elevate man to Heaven by offering grace through the sacraments of the Church.

Puritanism, on the other hand, assumed that grace and nature were two theaters of one Divine plan, each distinct and yet each involved with the other, incommensurate realms held in dialectical tension, inextricably entwined, wrestling in the universe and in the souls of men. This attitude is summed up in the title of one of Sibbes's works: *The Soul's Conflict with Itself and Victory over Itself by Faith.* If anything, God and grace were nearer to the Puritan than to the Anglican. My interpretation complicates the issue, but, I believe, offers firmer ground than Usher's for proving that Anglicanism was a religion of aspiration, and Puritanism of perspiration.

As our major interpretations differ, so do our minor ones. My understanding of the Puritans' eschatology encounters Usher's head-on. Usher, commenting on the Puritan's belief in predestination, wrote, "Which was his fate he did not know and the suspense tortured him."[4] In other words, uncertainty was the source of Puritanism's rigorous ethic. In my opinion, the reverse was true: the Puritan was objectively and subjectively certain of his salvation, and the assurance of it filled him with a gratitude that gave him the strength to glorify God. Yet though our conclusions differ broadly,[5] our points of departure are alike—we both take Baxter's thesis seriously, that fundamentals in religion were the life of the superstructure.

Recently a book has appeared whose conclusions are diametrically opposed to these. In view of such complete disagreement, I should perhaps take up the authors' findings in some detail. Charles and Katharine George's *The Protestant Mind,* an original and in many ways perceptive work, suffers from one serious defect: an unwillingness on the part of the authors to admit theological distinctions between Anglican and Puritan. Granted there are broad doctrinal agreements that establish the unequivocal Protestantism of Anglicanism—the rejection of papal supremacy, justification by faith, sacramental doctrine, the desire for a church-type Church—there still remain significant disagreements. The evidence presented in the preceding pages should have established this. Professor and Mrs. George examine sin, faith, and predestination, which they take to be "the very core" of the Anglican and Puritan creeds, and find essential agreement.[6] I have examined man, the Church, sacramental faith, and human destiny, and found substantial differences; and I have relegated predestination to a secondary position.

The Georges tend to dismiss Puritan-Anglican bickerings over the Prayer Book, abuses in the Church, ceremonies, and even Church government as trivial. An example in point is the cursory treatment given to the Whitgift-Cartwright dispute and the Admonition controversy, the discussion being followed by an invitation "to return to the mainstream of English political thought."[7] This is a grave misassessment of the material, for the Admonition controversy straddled the central years of Elizabethan ecclesiastical disharmony and encompassed the critical issues of both the past and the future. It was waged by the most eminent representatives of either side: Whitgift, Elizabeth's "black husband" and her favorite archbishop, and Cartwright, the Cambridge Professor of Divinity whom A. F. Scott Pearson described as "the representative Puritan."[8] The importance of the debate cannot be overemphasized; as W. H. Frere pointed out, although in bulk and volume much was added later, "the Puritan controversy did not really advance an inch beyond the point reached here."[9]

According to the Georges, Puritans and Anglicans clung to the *via media*. By this term they apparently mean that most Puritans and Anglicans wanted to retain a comprehensive Church, a judgment with which nobody could quarrel.[10] What is questionable is the use of the phrase *via media,* since it leads to the conclusion that Puritanism had little or nothing to do with the gestation of the Civil War: "The dynamic of what was to come in England must surely be sought, we feel, somewhere other than here."[11] This conclusion casts the vast bulk of past and present scholarship into limbo: for, with varying degrees of emphasis, all the great authorities from S. R. Gardiner to Christopher Hill have recognized the connection between Puritanism and the coming of the Civil War. Moreover, recent studies of the members of the Long Parliament have confirmed the generalization that Anglicans cleaved to the Crown and Puritans supported the

Parliament.[12] Whether this fact is intrinsically important or not, it demands serious consideration if not an attempt at explanation.

To return to our main argument: as was said, the disparity between Anglican and Puritan attitudes is most apparent in Hooker. The brilliance of his intellect, however, frustrated his greater purpose. Precisely because he defined general principles so clearly, he not only failed to overcome Puritanism, but brought the divergence of opinion into greater prominence. Whitgift had started with the same assumptions as Hooker, yet in the course of the controversy they had become submerged under particular issues. Thus Whitgift and Cartwright finished as firm friends (according to Whitgift's biographer George Paule), whereas Hooker and Travers never came to terms.[13] Unwittingly, Hooker contributed to increasing the stresses within the Church. Before the appearance of his *Ecclesiastical Polity,* there was some chance of agreement; after it there was none. We think of the lines from Purcell's *Dido and Aeneas:*

> Great minds against themselves conspire
> To shun the cure they most desire.

Not all prelates are as easy to "type" as Hooker, for theological views were not often so clearly defined. Grindal illustrates the continual difficulty attending any attempt to classify Anglican and Puritan. He is alleged to have been tinged with Puritanism because he sympathized with the prophesying movement,* defending it before the Queen, and telling her that she should refer ecclesiastical questions to her clergy, just as points of law were sent to the judges. As is well known, his stand on this point led to his suspension (1577). Grindal's Anglicanism, however, could never have been doubted if the whole incident had not been severed from the surrounding evidence and exaggerated beyond recognition. His regulations for the prophesyings, and his defense of them to the Queen, make it clear that his concern was to further the education of the clergy, and to silence criticism of

---

* "Prophesyings" were seminars in Biblical exegesis. They began to become popular among Puritan preachers in 1564, and the movement was at its peak in 1576, when Elizabeth ordered it suppressed.

the Establishment at the same time.[14] He valued learning for its own sake, a thoroughly Anglican characteristic based upon trust in the rational capacity of fallen man. He sympathized with prophesyings as accidental benefits; whereas the Puritans, who believed that faith was imparted primarily by the agency of preaching and only secondarily by means of the sacraments, considered them of central importance.

Again, Grindal's bold suggestion that the Queen refer ecclesiastical matters to her clergy did not trespass upon the ethic of absolute obedience. Elizabethan Anglicans joined that lesson to a constitutional theory of limited sovereignty, and Grindal merely extended current political theory to Church affairs. His offense lay not so much in the advice he gave, as in the bluntness with which he gave it.[15]

Finally, we have the evidence of Grindal's writings. His emphasis on the sacraments and his assumptions about the order of grace over nature in *A Fruitful Dialogue Between Custom and Verity*,[16] his sensitivity to promises of ultimate mercy in the *Homily Concerning the Justice of God*,[17] his ethics as displayed in the articles and injunctions,[18] his heated disputes with the Puritans over what were to him "matters indifferent"[19]—all establish his Anglicanism beyond reasonable doubt.

Despite the difficulties, then, a workable, though not infallible, classification of Anglican and Puritan is possible. Moreover, in my view, the problem is best approached by referring to theology rather than to options in Church government, which, after all, were subsidiary to theology. To achieve results, however, we must look beyond the doctrines that were shared, and consider those that diverged. We must examine the statements about human depravity, for example, to discover whether man was fallen yet still rational, or depraved in every faculty (which is to ask whether God and natural man were assumed to be compatible or incompatible). The questions are not easy. Were grace and human nature hierarchically or dialectically arranged? Was the Church regarded as a visible institution or as a gathering of saints? Was grace expected wholly from the sacraments, or largely by way of a prevenient selection that was confirmed by subjective reception of the Word in preaching? Was eschatological hope or fear the prevailing outlook? Did ethics fall within the idealistic to lenient range, or were they at once practical and combative? Such terms of reference define Anglican and Puritan as religious psychologies, which is patently imprecise. Even so, this method of definition may prove more satisfying than assessing the parties in terms of their relevance to the royal supremacy.

The difference in the Anglican and Puritan religious psychologies stemmed from the different preoccupations of the two groups' founders. It is trite but true to say that the Edwardian Reformation managed in theology what the Henrician Reformation had achieved in politics: namely, the destruction of papal supremacy. This was, indeed, the conscious and deliberate aim of the English reformers, and to achieve it they invoked those Protestant doctrines that impaired the spiritual dominion of the Papal See. The theological denial of papal supremacy was reinforced with additional doctrines: justification by faith alone diminished the Church's power over a person's entrance into Heaven or Hell; the rejection of transubstantiation undermined the magic of the Mass; and the reduction in the number of sacraments lessened the spiritual sway of the priesthood. Anglicanism became Protestant—unequivocally and not superficially—as far as was necessary to solve its particular problems. Beyond that it did not go because it had no need to.

Thus an array of beliefs remained, as it were, untouched in the religious subconscious, continuing unquestioned and unchecked: belief in the innate rationality of fallen man, in a hierarchical relationship between grace and nature, in a sacramental way to Heaven, in eschatological beatitude. Anglicanism became an amalgam of certain Protestant doctrines and certain traditional attitudes, the latter usually being less clearly defined. So the Edwardian Reformation introduced the tension between neo-Thomistic and Reformation elements that has endured to the present day.

Hence the phrase *via media,* which we use casually to mean the retention of old forms and ceremonies, was in essence a far

more profound development, for it involved the welding of new
theological concepts onto old metaphysical ones. The *via media*
of order and ritual is but surface evidence of a deeper attempt
at synthesis.

Calvin's self-imposed task was an academic one: to construct
a theology on the framework of the Apostles' Creed.[20] Both by
training and by temperament he had been imbued with Luther's
sense of total sin, and we must accept this as given when we come
to assess the influence of the Apostles' Creed on the whole theology. Unlike Luther, whose thought advanced in fits and starts,
Calvin developed his ideas in relative isolation, and essentially
over a few years. That is to say, by both circumstance and intent
his theology formed a system. Generalizing from personal insight, Luther had bridged the gap between God and man by
trusting to the love and mercy of Christ; Calvin, on the other
hand, relied on the power and energy of God. In relation to
Luther, Calvin diluted Christ's compassion and magnified God's
omnipotence. This was due to the nature of his framework.
There is little in the Apostles' Creed of the mercy of Christ or
the righteousness of God; rather, God is the Almighty, Father
and Creator, an incommensurate Being who had been involved
with man historically at the Creation, in the Fall of Adam, and
by the redeeming mission of His Son, and was still involved with
him through the ceaseless activity of the Holy Ghost. The Creed
itself suggests Calvin's revolutionary juxtaposition of grace and
nature. Secluded circumstances and originality of mind made
for the imaginative leap; so did Calvin's drastic view of man, inherited from Luther. But the text of the Creed had pointed the
direction of the leap. To this extent Calvin's chosen purpose to
rediscover pure doctrine by systematic analysis of the Creed
called forth the answers he arrived at.

Given the presumption of total depravity, it is easy to see how
the Creed demanded an emphasis on the sovereignty of God and
the Judgment of Christ. But why, it may be asked, when Anglicans regarded sacraments as efficacious in themselves, should Calvin have made them dependent on the preaching of the Word,
and on prevenient grace. A close reading of Calvin shows that

he held sacraments to be dependent on "the Word," and that he used this term in at least two distinct senses: first, to mean God's will; and, second, to mean the Gospel, or, more precisely, the pure doctrine of the Gospel.[21]

Baptism turned on the Word in the first sense, on God's immutable will. God's omnipotence logically imposed this application of predestination, for if God was Almighty, He must have foreknown and forechosen His elect. Predestination was an unavoidable deduction from the major theological principle, and baptism depended on the Word in this sense of God's will.

The Lord's Supper was dependent for efficacy on the Word in the second sense: that is, it moved upon the reception of pure doctrine. "The principal thing recommended by our Lord," wrote Calvin, "is to celebrate the ordinance with true understanding. From this it follows that the essential part lies in the doctrine. This being taken away, it is only a frigid unavailing ceremony."[22] Eucharist depended upon the Word as the intelligible exposition of the Gospel.

By setting this condition, Calvin revealed the temper of his mind; for, in effect, he was binding the gracious activity of God to his own doctrinal interpretations, thereby committing the very impiety and blasphemy he discovered in others. He betrayed his human weakness—intellectual arrogance—and yet this was hardly avoidable, since the task he had set himself was to provide "a summary of religion in all its parts."

Anglicanism and Puritanism were inherited world views, substantially fashioned by the preoccupations of their founders. Inheritances are not fixed deposits: they grow and diminish with changing situations and events. Since, however, the approach of this study has been analytical rather than chronological, the problems of historical development, of the continuity and discontinuity of traditions, have been largely avoided. They are, I hope, another story. The narrow concern here has been to uncover the theoretic bases of two antagonistic bodies of opinion. The movement backwards and forwards, producing evidence without reference to the context or to the tide of events, was undertaken deliberately to enhance the argument that two unities of principle existed at the Settlement and lasted to the Civil War, and that they were very different entities throughout.

Particular phases of the Anglican-Puritan conflict descended from different philosophies of heaven and earth. Anglicans thought the surplice a fitting addition to the dignity of a priest, it being a traditional garment of no inherent demerit. But to Puritans, whose notion of depravity was much greater, any dignity added to man was an indignity against God, and furthermore the surplice had been smeared by Popish usage. Ecclesiastical government was justified by Anglicans at first in relativistic, then in absolute, terms. The arguments of both schools employed an assimilative rationality and a deference to tradition that derived from trust in men's natural faculties. Puritanism's form of Church government rested on an interpretation of the Scriptures that employed an alien view of fallen man, and an alien view of the Church as a receptacle for the converted. Anglican individuality and Puritan communalism emerged from opposing ideas of the Church. Whether discipline was interpreted as outward conformity or as doctrinal and personal purity depended on whether the Church was regarded as a visible or a spiritual body. Moreover, the forms of service, dominated either by the sacraments or by preaching, owed their differences to unequal expectations of the approach of grace in the sacraments. Distinctive ethical systems stemmed from these ideas, and from different conceptions of the Last Judgment. In the 1630's, the Laudian innovations, in some respects insignificant enough, were symbols of fundamental assumptions that were more clearly felt than articulated.

In the common Anglican-Puritan doctrine of the sacraments, the elements were accounted signs of invisible grace. Similarly, in the Anglican-Puritan conflict, the visible clashes were signs of intangible, but vital, theological beliefs.

Notes

Notes

*The spelling of the titles of all books and other works
has been modernized throughout.*

Chapter 1

1. *The Prayer Book of Queen Elizabeth* (Edinburgh, 1911), p. 54.
2. Hugh Latimer, *Sermons by Hugh Latimer,* ed. G. E. Corrie, 2 vols. (Cambridge: Parker Society, 1844–45), I, 383.
3. Lancelot Andrewes, *Works,* 11 vols. (Oxford: Library of Anglo-Catholic Theology, 1878–80), I, 4–5.
4. Edwin Sandys, *The Sermons of Edwin Sandys,* ed. John Ayre (Cambridge: Parker Society, 1841), p. 133.
5. John Jewel, *The Works of John Jewel,* ed. John Ayre, 4 vols. (Cambridge: Parker Society, 1845–50), I, 100; III, 199.
6. Sandys, *Sermons,* p. 21.
7. Thomas Cranmer, *Works of Thomas Cranmer,* ed. J. E. Cox, 2 vols. (Cambridge: Parker Society, 1844–46), II, 143.
8. John Calvin, *Institutes of the Christian Religion,* trans. Henry Beveridge, 2 vols. (Edinburgh, 1875), II, ii, 13–14.
9. John Calvin, *Letters,* ed. J. Bonnet, 4 vols. (Philadelphia, n.d.), II, 189. To Protector Somerset, 22 Oct. 1548.
10. John Calvin, *Commentaries on the Epistle of Paul the Apostle to the Romans,* trans. John Owen (Edinburgh, 1849), Rom. vii. 14; also Calvin, *Institutes,* II, iii, 1, and IV, xv, 10.
11. John Strype, *The Life and Acts of John Whitgift,* 3 vols. (Oxford, 1822), II, 299.
12. Jewel, *Works,* III, 199.
13. Andrewes, *Works,* I, 5.
14. William Laud, *The Works of . . . William Laud, Sometime Lord Archbishop of Canterbury,* ed. William Scott and James Bliss, 7 vols. (Oxford: Library of Anglo-Catholic Theology, 1847–60), II, 71–72.
15. William Perkins, *The Works of That Famous and Worthy Minister of Christ in the University of Cambridge,* 3 vols. (London, 1616–18), I, 18.
16. *Ibid.,* p. 165.
17. Richard Rogers, *A Garden of Spiritual Flowers Planted by Ri. Ro., Will. Per., R. Green., M.M., and Geo. Web.* (London, 1610), Pt. 2, sig. A₂.
18. Calvin, *Institutes,* II, ii, 10; also II, v, 19.
19. Rogers, *A Garden of Spiritual Flowers,* Pt. 1, sig. D₂.
20. Thomas Adams, *The Works of T. Adams Being the Sum of His Sermons* (London, 1629), p. 62.
21. John Whitgift, *The Works of John Whitgift,* ed. John Ayre, 3 vols. (Cambridge: Parker Society, 1851–53), I, 191, n. 7.

22. Benjamin Whichcote, *Moral and Religious Aphorisms* (London, 1753), pp. 1–134.

23. A. S. P. Woodhouse, *Puritanism and Liberty* (London and Chicago, 1950); also Thomas Carlyle, ed., *Letters and Speeches of Oliver Cromwell,* 3 vols. (London, 1904), and W. C. Abbott, ed., *The Writings and Speeches of Oliver Cromwell,* 4 vols. (Cambridge, Mass., 1937–47).

24. Letter to Col. Hammond, 25 Nov. 1648, in Abbott, *Writings and Speeches,* I, 696.

25. Cranmer, *Works,* I, 225.

26. Richard Hooker, *Ecclesiastical Polity,* III, viii, 6, in *Works,* ed. John Keble, 2 vols. (Oxford, 1850).

27. Jewel, *Works,* I, 501.

28. John Donne, *Essays in Divinity,* ed. E. M. Simpson (Oxford, 1952), p. 56.

29. See, e.g., J. E. Neale, *Essays in Elizabethan History* (New York, 1959), pp. 114–16.

30. Andrewes, *Works,* VI, 290.

31. *Ibid.,* II, 380–81.

32. Laud, *Works,* II, 280.

33. Strype, *Whitgift,* II, 280; Thomas Fuller, *The Church History of Britain: From the Birth of Jesus Christ Until the Year 1648,* ed. J. S. Brewer, 6 vols. (Oxford, 1845), IV, 220.

34. Andrewes, "Judgement of the Lambeth Articles," in *Works,* VI, 289–300. Andrewes' opinion is congruent with the famous doctrinal statement of the Dutch Arminians, the Remonstrance to the States (1610). See also "The Tenets of the Arminians," in James Nichols, *Calvinism and Arminianism Compared in Their Principles and Tendency,* 2 vols. (London, 1824), Vol. I, Pt. 1, pp. 91–150.

35. There is a suggestive piece of evidence in Strype, *Whitgift,* II, 228 and 303. If it is to be trusted, perhaps we should discard the idea of the rise of Puritanism and talk, instead, of a delayed surge of Puritanism. According to Strype, "Calvin that great foreign reformer, his way of explaining the divine decree of predestination was not entertained by many learned men in the University of Cambridge. But, out of veneration for the man, that had deserved so well of the church of Christ, it now about the latter time of the Queen's reign, prevailed strongly then." In this case, the Protestant martyr John Hooper may have been an Arminian before Arminius. See Traheron to Bullinger, 10 Sept. 1552, and 3 June 1553, in H. Robinson, ed., *Original Letters Relative to the English Reformation,* 2 vols. (Cambridge: Parker Society, 1846–47), I, 324–28. The University controversy is discussed at length in Strype, *Whitgift,* II, 227–319.

36. Compare Nichols, *Calvinism and Arminianism,* Vol. I, Pt. 1, p. 124, tenet 4, with John Owen, "A Display of Arminianism," in *The Works of John Owen,* ed. William Orme, 21 vols. (London, 1826), Vol. V, Ch. 1.

William Prynne, in *The Church of England's Old Antithesis to New Arminianism* (London, 1629), dextrously slides Arminianism through Semi-Pelagianism, Pelagianism, and Socinianism to Popery!

37. R. L. Ollard, *Dictionary of English Church History* (London, 1919), p. 28.

38. Nichols, *Calvinism and Arminianism*, Vol. I, Pt. 1, p. 327n.

39. Laud, *Works*, III, 305.

40. John Rushworth, *Historical Collections*, 7 vols. (London, 1659–70), I, 660.

41. This disagrees with Godfrey Davies, "Arminianism versus Puritanism in England, ca. 1620–1640," in *Huntington Library Bulletin*, No. 5 (1934), p. 158, n. 5. For Prynne, the rejection of double predestination was an indication of more pernicious habits, and these disturbed him more than theological Arminianism. His plea to the bishops, in *The Church of England's Old Antithesis*, reveals the true source of his disquiet, for he begged them to use their powers to extirpate "all Semi-Pelagian Errors, and Arminian Novelties; all grace-defeating, all church-molesting Heresies, with their chief Fomenters: all late-erected Altars, Images, Tapers, Crucifixes, Duckings, Genuflexions, Eastern, yea Altar, adorations."

42. Calvin, *Institutes*, III, xxi, 1; also III, xxiii, 12.

43. Perkins, *Works*, II, 606.

44. *Ibid.*, I, 114.

45. Calvin, *Letters*, II, 189–90, 22 Oct. 1548.

46. Calvin, *Institutes*, III, xxiii, 14.

47. A. Scott Pearson, *Thomas Cartwright and Elizabethan Puritanism, 1535–1603* (Cambridge, 1925), p. 407. For Whitgift, see Sidney Lee in the *Dictionary of National Biography*; W. F. Hook, *Lives of the Archbishops of Canterbury*, 12 vols. (London, 1860–84), Vol. X; and P. M. Dawley, *John Whitgift and the English Reformation* (New York, 1954).

48. Strype, *Whitgift*, II, 282.

49. Robert Burns, "Holy Willie's Prayer."

50. St. Augustine, *Enchiridion*, Ch. 29, in *The Library of Christian Classics*, 25 vols. (London, 1953–57), VII, 406.

51. *Ibid.*, p. 407.

52. For Jansenism in general, see A. de Meyer, *Les Premières Controverses Jansénistes en France, 1640–1649* (Louvain, 1919); Nigel Abercrombie, *The Origins of Jansenism* (Oxford, 1936); and James Hastings, ed., *Encyclopedia of Religion and Ethics*, 13 vols. (New York, 1908–26).

53. John Bunyan, *The Pilgrim's Progress*, in *The Entire Works of John Bunyan*, ed. Henry Stebbing, 4 vols. (London, 1862), II, 13.

54. Ernst Troeltsch, *The Social Teaching of the Christian Churches*, trans. Olive Wyon, 2 vols. (London, 1931), Vol. II, Ch. 3, secs. i, ii, and iv; Max Weber, *The Protestant Ethic and the Spirit of Capitalism*, trans. Talcott Parsons (London, 1930), pp. 109–10.

55. R. H. Tawney, *Religion and the Rise of Capitalism,* Pelican edition (London, 1948), p. 120.

56. William Haller, *The Rise of Puritanism* (New York, 1938), pp. 83 and 85; see also M. M. Knappen, *Tudor Puritanism: A Chapter in the History of Idealism* (Chicago, 1939), pp. 368–70.

57. Haller, *Rise of Puritanism,* p. 83: "Predestination is a concept which, especially in its postulates of an absolute human depravity and a purely arbitrary human redemption, has often seemed absurd to the common sense and abhorrent to the humanitarian sentiment of later generations."

58. Carlyle's titanic description of the Battle of Dunbar is in *Letters and Speeches,* II, 172–73.

59. John Downame, *The Christian Warfare* (London, 1604), Bk. 1, Ch. 2.

60. Thomas Cartwright, *A Commentary upon the Epistle of St. Paul Written to the Colossians,* bound with Henry Airay, *Lectures upon the Whole Epistle of St. Paul to the Philippians* (Edinburgh and London, 1864), Col. i. 23–29.

61. Logan Pearsall Smith, ed., *Donne's Sermons: Selected Passages* (Oxford, 1932), p. 129.

62. G. Keynes, ed., *Ten Sermons by John Donne* (Soho, 1923), p. 106.

63. Hooker, *Works,* II, 691–92; his statements need careful unraveling.

64. Travers' "Supplication to Council," in *ibid.,* pp. 662–63.

65. Whitgift, *Works,* I, 184.

66. *Ibid.,* p. 458.

67. R. G. Usher, *The Presbyterian Movement in the Reign of Queen Elizabeth as Illustrated by the Minute Book of the Dedham Classis, 1582–1589,* Camden Society, Third Series, Vol. VIII; Ordinance for Church Government of 29 Aug. 1648, in C. H. Firth and R. S. Rait, eds., *Acts and Ordinances of the Interregnum,* 2 vols. (London, 1911), I, 1206; Laud, *Works,* V, 392.

68. Cf. Edmund Grindal, *Remains,* ed. W. Nicholson (Cambridge: Parker Society, 1843), p. 143.

69. Smith, *Donne's Sermons,* p. 87.

70. Lucy Hutchinson, *Memoirs of the Life of Col. John Hutchinson,* ed. C. H. Firth, 2 vols. (London, 1888), I, 78.

71. Tawney, *Religion and the Rise of Capitalism,* pp. 197–211.

72. Samuel Ward's *Diary* seems a caricature of Puritanism's Spartan characteristics. Ward makes the following confessions:

"[Undated]. Pride. Desire of vain glory, yes, in little things. . . . No delight in hearing God's word, or in prayer, or in receiving of the sacraments. Shame in serving God.

"May 13, 1595. My little pity of the boy who was whipped in the hall. My desire of preferment overmuch. My adulterous dream.

"May 16, 1595. Thy wandering mind in the chapel at prayer time.

"May 17, 1595. Thy wandering mind on herbals at prayer time, and at common place. Also thy gluttony the night before.

"May 19, 1595. The impatience in respect of thy disease. . . .

"May 22, 1595. My pride, which I took in every little action. . . .

"May 23, 1595. . . . My sleeping without remembering my last thought, which should have been of God.

"May 27, 1595. Thy overmuch delight in these transitory pleasures of this world."

The full text is in M. M. Knappen, *Two Elizabethan Puritan Diaries* (Chicago, 1933), pp. 103–5.

73. John Milton, *Areopagitica,* in *Works,* ed. Frank Allen Patterson, 18 vols. (New York, 1931–38), IV, 340.

74. Walter Travers, *A Directory of Church Government, Anciently Contended for* . . . (London, 1644).

75. William Prynne, *Histriomastix. The Player's Scourge, or, Actor's Tragedy, Divided in Two Parts* (London, 1633), Epistle Dedicatory.

76. Robert Browne, *A Treatise of Reformation Without Tarrying for Any, and of the Wickedness of Those Preachers Which Will Not Reform till the Magistrate Command or Compel Them* (1582). Reprinted in *Congregational Historical Society Transactions,* December 1901; also in Albert Peel and L. H. Carson, eds., *The Writings of Robert Harrison and Robert Browne* (London, 1953). Actually Browne's treatise exaggerated Puritans' tendencies; he was a Separatist.

77. Whitgift, *Works,* I, 3–12; Hooker, *Works,* I, 85–143.

78. James Ussher, *The Whole Works of the Most Reverend James Ussher,* ed. C. R. Elrington and J. M. Todd, 17 vols. (Dublin, 1847–64), XIII, 347–48.

79. See especially Hooker, *Ecclesiastical Polity,* I, i–viii.

80. Prov. xx. 27. On the Cambridge Platonists, see W. C. de Pauley, *The Candle of the Lord: Studies in the Cambridge Platonists* (London, 1937); Ernst Cassirer, *The Platonic Renaissance in England,* trans. J. P. Pettegrove (Edinburgh, 1953); Rosalie L. Colie, *Light and Enlightenment: A Study of the Cambridge Platonists and the Dutch Arminians* (Cambridge, 1957); and G. P. H. Pawson, *The Cambridge Platonists* (London, 1931).

81. Whitgift, *Works,* I, 190.

82. *Ibid.,* p. 187.

83. *Ibid.,* p. 190.

84. Richard Baxter, *Christian Directory: Christian Politics,* in *The Practical Works of the Rev. Richard Baxter,* ed. William Orme, 23 vols. (London, 1880), VI, 7.

85. Richard Baxter, *The Saints' Everlasting Rest,* Preface to Pt. 2, in *Works,* XXII, 239.

86. Baxter, *Christian Directory,* in *Works,* VI, 7.

87. Hooker, *Ecclesiastical Polity*, III, viii, 1–9; also *Works*, II, 393.
88. Thomas Burton, *The Diary of Thomas Burton, Esq.*, ed. J. T. Rutt, 4 vols. (London, 1828), I, lxix.
89. See below, Ch. 2.
90. E.g., Whitgift, *Works*, I, 175–295.

Chapter 2

1. Troeltsch, *Social Teaching*, II, 993.
2. Hooker, *Ecclesiastical Polity*, VIII, i, 2.
3. Directory for Public Worship, 4 Jan. 1644–45, in Firth and Rait, *Acts and Ordinances*, I, 584.
4. In Woodhouse, *Puritanism and Liberty*, pp. 125–78.
5. Daniel Neal, *History of the Puritans, or Protestant Nonconformists, from the Reformation in 1517 to the Revolution in 1688*, 5 vols. (London, 1822), Prefaces to Vols. I and III.
6. W. K. Jordan, *The Development of Religious Toleration in England, 1530–1640*, 3 vols. (London, 1938), Vol. I, Ch. 4.
7. Troeltsch, *Social Teaching*, II, 591.
8. Calvin, *Institutes*, IV, i, 3.
9. John Cotton, *The Way of the Churches of Christ in New England* (London, 1645), pp. 56 and 58; also quoted in Cotton's *God's Mercy Mixed with His Justice*, ed. E. H. Emerson (Gainesville, Fla., 1958), pp. x–xi. The third sermon in *God's Mercy*, which gives the book its title, deals with the same subject.
10. William Ames, *The Marrow of Sacred Divinity* (London, [1638?]), Ch. 29.
11. John Calvin, *Commentaries on the First Book of Moses, Called Genesis*, trans. J. King, 2 vols. (Edinburgh, 1847–50), Gen. i. 63.
12. Owen, *Works*, XIV, 130.
13. Calvin, *Commentaries on Genesis*, Gen. i. 65.
14. Owen, *Works*, XIV, 343–44.
15. Perkins, *Works*, II, 328 (Gal. v. 17).
16. *Ibid.*, III, 157 (Heb. i. 29).
17. Adams, *Works*, p. 66.
18. Whitgift, *Works*, I, 183–84.
19. See, e.g., *ibid.*, pp. 175–295.
20. W. M. Southgate, "The Marian Exiles and the Influence of John Calvin," in *History*, XXVII (1942), 148–52, offers a critical bibliographical sketch. I share his preference for R. W. Dixon's discussion, *History of the Church of England from the Abolition of the Roman Jurisdiction*, 6 vols. (London and Oxford, 1881–1902), Vol. IV, Ch. 29, as the most sympathetic account. Southgate, however, follows the orthodox view by stating without reserve that Elizabethan Anglicanism was thoroughly Calvinistic

in doctrine, although earlier he had noted that Bullinger and Calvin (i.e., Zurich and Geneva) did not always agree. This curious contradiction serves to illustrate how deep historical misconceptions are embedded. See my discussion of predestination in Chapter 1.

21. Grindal, *Remains*, p. 46.

22. Richard Field, *Of the Church* (Oxford, 1635), Bk. 1, Chs. 2 and 4.

23. Hooker, *Ecclesiastical Polity*, III, viii, 11.

24. *Ibid.*, p. 12.

25. *Ibid.*, p. 15.

26. See, e.g., Laud, *Works*, II, 307; P. E. More and F. L. Cross have gathered up some Anglican opinions on the invocation of the saints in *Anglicanism: The Thought and Practice of the Church of England Illustrated from the Religious Literature of the Seventeenth Century* (Milwaukee, Wis., 1935), pp. 254–56.

27. W. H. Frere and C. E. Douglas, eds., *Puritan Manifestoes* (London, 1907), p. 115.

28. *Ibid.*, pp. 11–12.

29. Whitgift, *Works*, III, 53.

30. Albert Peel, ed., *The Second Part of a Register*, 2 vols. (Cambridge, 1915), I, 95.

31. Frere and Douglas, *Puritan Manifestoes*, p. 13.

32. Whitgift, *Works*, III, 97.

33. Henry Gee and William Hardy, eds., *Documents Illustrative of English Church History* (London, 1896), p. 541 (sec. 16).

34. Calvin, *Institutes*, IV, i, 3.

35. Baxter, *Works*, XII, 355.

36. *Ibid.*, p. 13.

37. George Yule, *The Independents in the English Civil War* (Cambridge and Melbourne, 1958), Ch. 1.

38. Champlin Burrage, *The Early English Dissenters in the Light of Recent Research*, 2 vols. (Cambridge, 1912), II, 157.

39. Whitgift, *Works*, I, 22.

40. *Ibid.*, III, 295–96.

41. Woodhouse, *Puritanism and Liberty*, pp. 130–31; also William Bradshaw, "English Puritanism," in Burrage, *Early English Dissenters*, I, 288.

42. Woodhouse, *Puritanism and Liberty*, p. 139.

43. Whitgift, *Works*, I, 21–22.

44. *Ibid.*, III, 159.

45. Frere and Douglas, *Puritan Manifestoes*, p. 17.

46. Whitgift, *Works*, III, 266–67, 279.

47. Gee and Hardy, *Documents*, p. 510.

48. *Ibid.*, p. 543.

49. Weber, *The Protestant Ethic and the Spirit of Capitalism*; and Tawney, *Religion and the Rise of Capitalism*, Ch. 4, especially n. 32, pp. 311–13.

50. Woodhouse, *Puritanism and Liberty,* Introduction.

51. Perkins, *Works,* III, 157 (Heb. i. 29).

52. Richard Sibbes, *A Fountain Sealed: Or the Duty of the Sealed to the Spirit, and the Work of the Spirit in Sealing* (London, 1637), pp. 149, 233.

53. Whitgift, *Works,* I, 390.

54. Perry Miller and Thomas H. Johnson, eds., *The Puritans* (New York, 1938), pp. 209–10.

55. Speech II, 12, Sept. 1654, in Carlyle, *Letters & Speeches,* IV, 53.

56. Whitgift, *Works,* I, 458–59.

57. Hooker, *Ecclesiastical Polity,* III, ix, 2.

58. *Ibid.,* x, 1.

59. *Ibid.,* xi, 16.

60. Strype, *Whitgift,* I, 559–60; II, 48, 407. Bancroft's sermon is reprinted in George Hickes, *Bibliotheca scriptorum ecclesiae Anglicanae* (London, 1709), pp. 247–315.

61. John Strype, *Annals of the Reformation . . . ,* 4 vols. (Oxford, 1824), III, ii, 98.

62. Richard Bancroft, "Certain Slaunderous Speeches Against the Present Estate of the Church of England Published to the People of the Precisians," in Albert Peel, ed., *Tracts Ascribed to Richard Bancroft* (Cambridge, 1953), pp. 93–125.

63. Hooker, *Ecclesiastical Polity,* III, xi, 16.

64. John Cosin, for example, specifically opposed a strict doctrine of succession, resting his case on historical continuity and apostles' practice; see *The Works of John Cosin,* 5 vols. (Oxford: Library of Anglo-Catholic Theology, 1849–76), IV, 241 *et seq.* See also Field, *Of the Church,* Bk. 5, Chs. 25–27, pp. 488 *et seq.*

65. Laud, *Works,* Vol. VI, Pt. 1, p. 43.

66. Andrewes, *Works,* VI, 352.

67. Richard Montagu, *Origins Ecclesiastical,* II, 463, quoted in A. J. Mason, *The Church of England and Episcopacy* (Cambridge, 1914), p. 152. Taylor quoted Cyprian with approval: "If ye take away bishops, the Church . . . can no longer be called a church." *Episcopacy Asserted,* in *Works,* ed. Reginald Heber, 10 vols. (London, 1849–54), V, 193.

68. The relation between the Churches of Scotland and England in this period has received considerable attention: Norman Sykes, "The Church of England and the Non-Episcopal Churches in the Sixteenth and Seventeenth Centuries," in *Theology,* Occasional Paper, New Series, No. 11 (1948); Norman Sykes, correspondence in *Theology,* Jan. to Sept. 1949, where Sykes, Eric Kemp, and Gregory Dix differ; B. D. Till, "Episcopacy in the Works of Elizabethan and Caroline Divines," Ch. 4 in K. M. Carey, ed., *The Historic Episcopate* (London, 1954); Henry A. Wilson, *Episcopacy and Unity* (London and New York, 1912); E. T. Davies, *Episcopacy and the Royal Supremacy in the Church of England in the XVI Century*

(Oxford, 1950); H. F. Woodhouse, *The Doctrine of the Church of England in Anglican Theology, 1547–1603* (London, 1954); Paul A. Welsby, *Lancelot Andrewes, 1555–1626* (London, 1958), pp. 173 *et seq.*; Mason, *The Church of England and Episcopacy*; and A. L. Peck, *Anglicanism and Episcopacy* (London, 1958)—a high churchman's attack on Sykes's conclusions.

69. Richard Baxter, *Five Disputations of Church-Government and Worship* (London, 1659); also paraphrased in F. J. Powicke, *The Life of the Reverend Richard Baxter* (London, 1924), p. 271.

70. *Lambeth Conference: The Encyclical Letter from the Bishops Together with the Resolutions and Reports* (London, 1948), p. 50.

Chapter 3

1. Martyr on I Cor. ix. 3; quoted in Joseph C. McLelland, *The Visible Words of God* (London, 1957), p. 229.

2. According to Calvin, "the whole [doctrine of the Eucharist] was crowned by Peter Martyr who has left nothing to be desired." *Tracts,* trans. Henry Beveridge, 3 vols. (Edinburgh, 1844–45), II, 535.

3. Laud, *Works,* II, 306.

4. Perkins, *Works,* I, 558.

5. *Ibid.,* p. 509.

6. *Ibid.,* p. 196.

7. Jewel, *Works,* III, 620, and IV, 399; Laud, *Works,* II, 32.

8. Cranmer, *Works,* I, 288.

9. Perkins, *Works,* I, 313.

10. Cranmer, *Works,* I, 373; also 139, 219.

11. That Cranmer was Zwinglian is maintained currently by Gregory Dix, *The Shape of the Liturgy* (London, 1949), and W. Jardine Grisbrooke, ed., *Anglican Liturgies of the Seventeenth and Eighteenth Centuries* (London, 1958), pp. xii–xiii.

12. Calvin, *Tracts,* II, 238.

13. *Ibid.,* p. 506.

14. Article XXI; cf. David Laing, ed., *The Works of John Knox,* 6 vols. (Edinburgh, 1895), IV, 71–73.

15. The Directory is in Firth and Rait, *Acts and Ordinances,* I, 598. For the Savoy Declaration of 1658, see A. G. Matthews, ed., *The Savoy Declaration of Faith and Order* (London, 1958), p. 116, article 2.

16. Andrewes, *Works,* I, 213–14.

17. Owen, *Works,* pp. 17, 199.

18. Cosin, *Works,* V, 345.

19. Owen, *Works,* pp. 17, 199, 211.

20. Quoted in Stephen Neill, *Anglicanism* (London: Pelican, 1958), p. 94.

21. Andrewes, *Works,* III, 163.

22. Hooker, *Ecclesiastical Polity,* V, lvii, 4; Baxter, *Works,* XVI, 473.

23. C. W. Dugmore, *Eucharistic Doctrine in England from Hooker to Waterland* (London, 1942), Chs. 1, 2.

24. Laud, *Works,* II, 340–41.

25. Perkins, *Works,* I, 586.

26. Whitgift, *Works,* II, 521, 537.

27. Calvin, *Institutes,* IV, xv, 22.

28. Whitgift, *Works,* II, 525n.

29. *Ibid.,* pp. 537–38.

30. *Ibid.,* p. 538.

31. *Ibid.,* p. 537.

32. Hooker, *Ecclesiastical Polity,* V, lx, 3.

33. Frere and Douglas, *Puritan Manifestoes,* pp. 14, 97–98.

34. Whitgift, *Works,* I, 207–8; II, 525, 529, 537–39.

35. Hooker, *Ecclesiastical Polity,* V, lx, 2; see also Whitgift, *Works,* II, 538–39.

36. Whitgift, *Works,* II, 539.

37. *Ibid.,* I, 207 *et seq.*

38. Jewel, *Works,* II, 781.

39. Andrewes, *Works,* I, 282.

40. Calvin, *Tracts,* II, 152.

41. *Ibid.,* p. 53.

42. Baxter, *Works,* XV, 472–79.

43. Firth and Rait, *Acts and Ordinances,* I, 596–98.

44. W. D. Maxwell, *A History of Worship in the Church of Scotland* (London, 1955), pp. 125–26, 141.

45. Hooker, *Ecclesiastical Polity,* V, lxviii, 45, 48.

46. Frere and Douglas, *Puritan Manifestoes,* p. 14.

47. Whitgift, *Works,* II, 101 *et seq.*

48. *Ibid.,* p. 103.

49. Maxwell, *A History of Worship in the Church of Scotland,* pp. 136–37.

50. Laud, *Works,* VI, 57.

51. Whitgift, *Works,* II, 14 *et seq.*

52. *Ibid.,* III, 22.

53. Haller, *Rise of Puritanism,* p. 258.

54. Christopher Hill, *The Economic Problems of the Church from Archbishop Whitgift to the Long Parliament* (Oxford, 1956), pp. 108–9.

55. Whitgift, *Works,* II, 31.

56. Robert Steele, *Tudor and Stuart Proclamations, 1485–1714,* 2 vols. (Oxford, 1910), I, 208.

57. S. R. Gardiner, *A History of England from the Accession of James I to the Outbreak of the Civil War,* 10 vols. (London, 1884), VIII, 152.

58. John Bastwick, *The Litany of John Bastwick*, Vol. V in *A Collection of Scarce and Valuable Tracts . . . from Libraries . . . Particularly That of the Late Lord Somers*, ed. Walter Scott (London, 1810), pp. 407 *et seq.*

59. Laud, *Works*, VI, 59.

60. John Pearson, *An Exposition of the Creed* (London, 1676), pp. 305–6.

61. *Ibid.*, p. 304.

62. Latimer, *Sermons*, I, 11, 224.

63. Ussher, *Works*, XI, 195.

64. St. Augustine, *Enchiridion*, Ch. 29, in *Library of Christian Classics*, VII, 406–7.

65. Perkins, *Works*, I, 264–73.

66. *Ibid.*, p. 270.

67. John Calvin, *Commentaries on the Catholic Epistles*, trans. John Owen (Edinburgh, 1855), Jude, 15.

68. Calvin, *Institutes*, III, ii, 17. Also consider Edward Dering's view: "The judgement of God . . . pierces deeply into the hearts of true believers, and the word that they hear, it worketh mightily in them, more sharp than a two-edged sword; it entreth through them even to the dividing asunder of the soul and of the spirit, and of the joints, and of the marrow, and examineth all the thoughts and the intents of the heart, so that it is impossible that any part of them should be hid, but they are all open unto judgement, and hear the voice of the Lord. Then their sin is revived in the midst of their bowels, their conscience hath no rest, they feel death working in their hearts, and hell is before them. They see sin on the right hand, and Satan on their left, shame under their feet, and an angry Judge above them, the world full of destruction without, a worm gnawing the heart within: the poor Sinner knoweth not what to do. To hide himself is impossible, and to appear it is intolerable. When he breaketh out into loud cryings: O wretched man that I am, who shall deliver me from the body of this death: he giveth no rest unto his eyes, nor sleep unto his eyelids, until he find him that is able to save him from this wrath. In his bed by night he seeketh him whom his soul loveth: in the streets and open places he enquireth after him, and after many days in which he cannot find him, Christ showeth himself at the last a perpetual deliverer, a victorious Lion of the tribe of Judah, in whom he hath strong salvation. When he mourns, because of the plague that was before him, Christ will approach near, and wipe away the tears from his eyes." Edward Dering, *XXVII Lectures, for Readings, upon Part of the Epistle to the Hebrews* (London, 1576), Heb. v. 8–9; cf. Robert Bolton, "Of Judgement," in *Mr. Bolton's Last and Learned Work of the Last Four Things* (London, 1635). Dering's allegory emphasizes the point that the nightmare (with its happy ending) occurred to true believers.

69. Smith, *Donne's Sermons,* p. 216. See also Sermons VII, XXIII, and XIV, and Six Sermons, II, in *ibid.*

70. *Ibid.,* pp. 217–19.

Chapter 4

1. Christopher Hill, "Protestantism and the Rise of Capitalism," in F. J. Fisher, ed., *Essays in the Economic and Social History of Tudor and Stuart England* (Cambridge, 1961), pp. 15 *et seq.*

2. John Woolton, *The Christian Manual* (Cambridge: Parker Society, 1851), p. 5.

3. John Norden, *A Progress of Piety* (Cambridge: Parker Society, 1847), pp. 36, 71.

4. Reinhold Niebuhr, *The Nature and Destiny of Man,* 2 vols. (New York, 1945), II, 180.

5. Zinzendorf: "Nullam inhaerentem Perfectionem in hac vita agnosco. Est hic Error Errorum. Eum per totem orbem igne et gladio persequor, conculco, ad internecionem do. Christus est sola Perfectio nostra. Qui Perfectionem inhaerentem sequitur, Christum denegat."

Wesley: "Ego vero credo, Spiritum Christi operari Perfectionem in vere Christianis." John Wesley, *The Journal of the Rev. John Wesley,* 4 vols. (London, 1906), I, 324.

6. George Herbert, *The Poetical Works of George Herbert,* ed. A. B. Grossart (London, 1891), p. 230, stanzas 2 and 6.

7. Woolton, *The Christian Manual,* p. 97.

8. Lam. ii. 9.

9. Milton, *Areopagitica,* in *Works,* IV, 311.

10. Bunyan, *The Pilgrim's Progress,* in *Works,* II, 127, stanzas 1 and 3.

11. Hill, *Economic Problems of the Church,* p. 237, n. 1.

12. R. G. Usher, *The Reconstruction of the English Church,* 2 vols. (New York and London, 1910), I, 211; Hill, *Economic Problems of the Church,* p. 226, regards this as an underestimate.

13. In Gee and Hardy, *Documents,* pp. 508 *et seq.* and 537 *et seq.*

14. Whitgift, *Works,* I, 528–29.

15. Hill, *Economic Problems of the Church,* p. 226. The 1604 Canon is in David Wilkins, *Concilia Magnae Britanniae et Hiberniae . . . ,* 4 vols. (London, 1737), IV, 388.

16. *Certain Homilies, to be Read in Churches, in the Time of Queen Elizabeth . . . to Which are Added the Thirty-Nine Articles of the United Church of England and Ireland: and the Constitution and Canons Ecclesiastical* (Dublin, 1824), pp. 105, 109–10.

17. Sandys, *Sermons,* p. 198.

18. Hooker, *Ecclesiastical Polity,* I, viii; VIII, vi.

19. C. H. McIlwain, ed., *The Political Works of James I* (Cambridge, Mass., 1918), p. 307.

20. *Ibid.,* pp. 205–6.

21. See W. H. Greenleaf, "James I and the Divine Right of Kings," in *Political Studies,* Vol. V (1957), No. 1.

22. Robert Filmer, *Patriarcha and Other Political Works,* ed. Peter Laslett (Oxford, 1949), p. 229.

23. See Gerald Straka, "The Final Phase of the Divine Right Theory in England, 1688–1702," in *English Historical Review,* Vol. LXXVII (October 1962).

24. Jasper Ridley, *Thomas Cranmer* (Oxford, 1962), p. 12, and Ch. 24.

25. Calvin, *Institutes,* IV, xx, 32.

26. Aphorism 100.

27. See John T. McNeill, "The Democratic Element in Calvin's Thought," in *Church History,* Vol. XVIII (1949), No. 3; and Hans Baron, Calvinist Republicanism and Its Historical Roots," in *ibid.,* Vol. VIII (1939), No. 1.

28. Perkins, *A Treatise of Conscience,* in *Works,* I, 530.

29. Henry Smith, "The Magistrates' Scripture," in *The Sermons* (London, 1593), p. 710.

30. Edward Dering, *A Sermon Preached Before the Queen's Majesty, the 25 Day of February . . . in Anno 1569* (London, 1569).

31. John Eliot, *De Jure Maiestatis,* quoted in Harold Hulme, *The Life of Sir John Eliot, 1592–1632* (New York, 1957), p. 376.

32. Milton, *The Tenure of Kings and Magistrates,* in *Works,* V, 50.

33. Bulstrode Whitelock, *Memorials of the English Affairs,* 4 vols. (Oxford, 1853), III, 374.

34. Leonard J. Trinterud, "The Origins of Puritanism," in *Church History,* XX (1951), 55 and 57, n. 42.

35. Calvin, *Institutes,* II, ix, 4; II, x, 1.

36. Calvin, *Commentaries on Genesis,* Gen. xvii. 2.

37. "W. T. to the Reader," in William Tyndale, *The New Testament,* ed. N. Hardy Wallis (Cambridge, 1938).

38. See especially John Calvin, *Commentaries on the Book of the Prophet Isaiah,* trans. William Pringle, 4 vols. (Edinburgh, 1850–53), Isa. lv. 3.

39. Perry Miller, "The Marrow of Puritan Divinity," in *Publications of the Colonial Society of Massachusetts,* Vol. XXXII, 1937. Professor Miller made too much of the differences; yet he was right to trace the origins of New England Puritanism to Perkins and Ames, and before them to Calvin; and there is evidence of theological Arminianism in such a Puritan as Richard Baxter. God's promises stood forever, but at some point Christ offered himself to the believer, who, to cement the covenant,

had to assent freely with his will to love and obey God. At the same time, faith was "wrought in [the believer] by the Word and Spirit of Christ." For the giving of Himself by Christ there was a willingness offered up by the saved person. In this sense the covenant was mutual.

This subtle doctrine seems to allow the individual a consenting prerogative, while it gives the credit for faith to the Holy Spirit. It is a variation whose significance can be overblown if one exaggerates the importance that Calvin attached to double predestination. When Calvin's theology was carried into everyday parish life—particularly by such an ecumenicalist as Baxter—such a development was inevitable; the *decretum horribile* does not serve the needs of practical pastoral ministry very well. Baxter's deviation, however, was consistent not only with the activism that Calvin's doctrine of man encouraged so heartily, but also with the Puritan belief in the immutability of God's decrees and testament; in other words, his position represented a very understandable progression from the magisterial reformer's views, and not an abandonment of them. Richard Baxter, *The Practical Works of the Late Reverend and Pious Mr. Richard Baxter,* 4 vols. (London, 1707), III, 63, 556; IV, 157.

40. John Preston, *The Doctrine of the Saints' Infirmities* (London, 1638), p. 36.

41. *Ibid.,* p. 38.

42. John Preston, *Life Eternal, or a Treatise of the Knowledge of the Divine Essence and Attributes* (London, 1634), pp. 84–85.

43. Miller's views have been extended almost beyond recognition by Trinterud, and Miller's views, if not Trinterud's, seem to have been absorbed by Jerald C. Brauer, "Reflections on the Nature of English Puritanism," in *Church History,* XXIII (1954), 99–108.

44. Dudley Fenner, *The Whole Doctrine of the Sacraments* (Middleburg, 1588), pp. 118, 137, 160.

45. After *Sacra Theologica* (London, 1585), Fenner's three main doctrinal works are *Certain Godly and Learned Treatises* (Edinburgh, 1592), *The Grounds of Religion Set Down . . .* (Middleburg, 1587), and *The Whole Doctrine of the Sacraments.* For Cotton's ideas, see his *Covenant of God's Free Grace* (London, 1645). Cotton's covenant theology was complex. He retained a Calvinistic core—God offering promises and requiring the duty of obedience—but he thought man could depart from God, and sometimes needed to reaffirm his profession of faith. To this was wedded a visible and mutual covenant with a congregation to enter the visible Church. Cotton's additions to Calvin's ideas exemplify his proximity to Separatism; see *The Way of the Churches of Christ in New England.*

46. Knappen, *Tudor Puritanism,* p. 376.

47. R. W. K. Hinton, "English Constitutional Theories from Sir John

Fortescue to Sir John Eliot," in *English Historical Review*, Vol. LXXV (July 1960).

48. Champlin Burrage, *The Church Covenant Idea* (Philadelphia, 1904).

49. Milton, *The Tenure of Kings and Magistrates*, in *Works*, V, 35.

50. Sidney A. Burrell describes the development of covenant organizations in Scotland in "The Covenant Idea as a Revolutionary Symbol: Scotland, 1596–1637," in *Church History*, Vol. XXVII (June 1958).

51. Robert Browne, *A Book Which Showeth the Life and Manners of All True Christians* (Middleburg, 1582), and *An Answer to Master Cartwright for His Letter for Joining with the English Church* (London, 1583).

52. George L. Mosse, *The Holy Pretence: A Study in Christianity and Reason of State from William Perkins to John Winthrop* (Oxford, 1957), Chs. 4 and 5.

53. *Ibid.*, pp. 133, 136.

54. Thomas Fuller, *The Holy and Profane States* (London, 1884), pp. 170–71.

55. For a brilliant attempt to apply the last definition to seventeenth-century political theory, see C. B. Macpherson, *The Political Theory of Possessive Individualism* (Oxford, 1962).

56. The main contributions to the controversy, roughly arranged in order of appearance, are as follows: Weber, *The Protestant Ethic and the Spirit of Capitalism*; Troeltsch, *The Social Teaching of the Christian Churches*; Werner Sombart, *The Quintessence of Capitalism*, trans. M. Epstein (London, 1915); Lujo Brentano, *Die Anfänge des Kapitalismus* (Munich, 1916); R. H. Tawney's Introduction to Thomas Wilson, *A Discourse upon Usury* (London, 1925), "A propos des idées économiques de Calvin," in *Mélanges d'histoire offerts à Henri Pirenne . . .* (Brussels, 1926); Henri Hauser, *Les Débuts de capitalisme* (Paris, 1927); Tawney, *Religion and the Rise of Capitalism*; Henri Sée, *Modern Capitalism: Its Origin and Evolution*, trans. Homer B. Vanderblue and Georges F. Doriot (New York, 1928); Georgia Harkness, *John Calvin: The Man and His Ethics* (New York, 1931); H. M. Robertson, *Aspects of the Rise of Economic Individualism* (Cambridge, 1933); James Brodrick, *The Economic Morals of the Jesuits: An Answer to Dr. H. M. Robertson* (London, 1934); Conrad H. Moehlmann, "The Christianization of Interest," in *Church History*, Vol. III (1934); "L'Economie calvinienne," in *Etudes sur Calvin et le calvinisme* (Paris, 1935); Albert Hyma, *Christianity, Capitalism, and Communism* (Ann Arbor, Mich., 1937), "Calvinism and Capitalism in the Dutch Netherlands, 1555–1706," in *Journal of Modern History*, Vol. X (1938), and *Renaissance to Reformation* (Grand Rapids, Mich., 1951); Talcott Parsons, *The Structure of Social Action* (New York, 1937); André

Sayous, "Calvinisme et capitalisme: L'Expérience genevoise," in *Annales d'Histoire Economique et Sociale,* Vol. VII (1938); Carl F. Taeusch, "History of the Concept of Usury," in *Journal of the History of Ideas,* Vol. III (June 1942); Winthrop H. Hudson, "Puritanism and the Spirit of Capitalism," in *Church History,* Vol. XVIII (March 1949); Benjamin H. Nelson, *The Idea of Usury* (Princeton, N.J., 1949); Amintore Fanfani, *Catholicism, Protestantism, and Capitalism* (New York, 1955); John T. Noonan, *The Scholastic Analysis of Usury* (Cambridge, Mass., 1957); Charles George, "English Calvinist Opinion on Usury, 1600–1640," in *Journal of the History of Ideas,* Vol. XVIII (October 1957); and André Biéler, *La Pensée économique et sociale de Calvin* (Geneva, 1959).

57. Biéler, *La Pensée économique,* pp. 166 *et seq.*

58. Introduction to Wilson, *Discourse upon Usury,* pp. 112–13.

59. Jewel, "Commentary upon I Thessalonians iv. 6," in *Works,* II, 851.

60. John Blaxton, *The English Usurer, or Usury Condemned by the Most Learned and Famous Divines of the Church of England* (Oxford, 1634).

61. Thomas Culpepper, *A Tract Against Usury* (London, 1621). See also Nicholas Heming, *A Godly Treatise Concerning the Lawful Uses of Riches,* trans. from Heming's Latin by Thomas Rogers (London, 1598); and Miles Mosse, *The Arraignment and Conviction of Usury* (London, 1598).

62. Robert Bolton, *A Short and Private Discourse Between Mr. Bolton and One M.S. Concerning Usury* (London, 1637); cf. Roger Fenton, *A Treatise of Usury* (London, 1611). Bolton would allow a "liberal" usury (i.e., a return that had not been bargained for beforehand) and a "recompensing" usury (i.e., a return for loss suffered by gain ceasing or damage occurring because of the loan of the capital). Cf. Jewel, *Works,* II, 856–58.

63. Henry Smith, *The Works,* 2 vols. (London, 1886–87), I, 97–98.

64. Perkins, *Works,* I, 63–64; see also Ames, *The Marrow of Sacred Divinity,* Bk. 2, Ch. 20.

65. Robertson, *Aspects of the Rise of Economic Individualism,* and Hudson, "Puritanism and the Spirit of Capitalism," in *Church History,* Vol. XVIII (March 1949).

66. 13 Eliz. c. 8; reinstating parts of 37 Hen. VIII c. 9.

67. 21 Jac. I c. 17.

68. Simonds D'Ewes, *The Journal of All the Parliaments During the Reign of Queen Elizabeth* (London, 1682), pp. 172–74.

69. *Ibid.,* p. 174.

70. Tawney, *Religion and the Rise of Capitalism,* pp. 178, 212.

71. Hooker, *Ecclesiastical Polity,* V, lxxiv, 1; Herbert, *Works,* pp. 236–37; Cosin, *Works,* I, 56; Fuller, *The Holy and Profane States,* pp. 55–56.

72. Thomas Gataker, *A Good Wife, God's Gift* (London, 1620), p. 166;

Smith, "A Preparative for Marriage," in *Sermons,* pp. 1 *et seq.*; Perkins, *Works,* II, 670–71; Adams, *Works,* p. 1234. Puritans were even apt to insert pleas for marriage into discussions of Christ's virgin birth!

73. Joseph Hall, *Works,* ed. Peter Wynter, 10 vols. (London, 1863), VIII, 105.

Conclusion

1. Baxter, *Works* (1880), XVII, 341.
2. A. S. P. Woodhouse, "Religion and Some Foundations of English Democracy," in *Philosophical Review,* LXI (1952), 513.
3. Usher, *Reconstruction of the English Church,* I, 77–78.
4. *Ibid.,* p. 79.
5. Usher's sympathies are entirely with Bancroft—witness the chapter title "Unmasking the Puritans," and the title of the whole work, *The Reconstruction of the English Church.* From another point of view, however, Bancroft's policy can be regarded as detrimental to the Establishment; for far from routing Puritanism, it had the effect of making the Puritans clarify their thinking. Puritanism's surge of moralism was less an index of defeat than a streamlining of its spirit. Usher emphasized the doctrine of predestination and Puritan individualism, both of which emphases I would modify, though not altogether deny.
6. Charles and Katharine George, *The Protestant Mind of the English Reformation, 1570–1640* (Princeton, N.J., 1961), p. 71.
7. *Ibid.,* p. 196.
8. Pearson, *Thomas Cartwright and Elizabethan Puritanism,* pp. 407–15.
9. W. H. Frere, *The English Church in the Reigns of Elizabeth and James I, 1558–1625* (London, 1904), p. 182. See also McGinn, *The Admonition Controversy,* Ch. IX.
10. George, *The Protestant Mind,* pp. 372–74.
11. *Ibid.,* p. 398.
12. Exceptions to the generalization were Bishop John Williams on one side and Sir Ralph Hopton on the other. See Douglas Brunton and D. H. Pennington, *Members of the Long Parliament* (London, 1954); Mary Keeler, *The Long Parliament, 1640–1641* (Philadelphia, 1954); and the additional notes in the Appendix of George Yule, *The Independents in the English Civil War* (Cambridge and Melbourne, 1958).
13. George Paule, *The Life of John Whitgift* (London, 1699), p. 71.
14. John Strype, *The History of the Life and Acts of Edmund Grindal* (Oxford, 1821), pp. 327, 568.
15. *Ibid.,* p. 571.
16. Grindal, *Remains,* pp. 39–74.

17. *Ibid.*, pp. 105–10.

18. *Ibid.*, pp. 132–44.

19. Strype, *Grindal,* pp. 170–76.

20. See Gaspar Olévian on the "Method and Arrangement or Subject of the Whole Work," in Calvin, *Institutes,* I, 27 *et seq.*

21. Calvin, *Institutes,* III, ii, 6; I, xi, 7; IV, xiv, 4.

22. Calvin, *Tracts,* II, 190.

Index

Index

Date Due